# LEVELING THE PLAYING FIELD

# Leveling the Playing Field

## Advancing Women in Jewish Organizational Life

**Shifra Bronznick**
Founder and President
Advancing Women Professionals
and the Jewish Community

**Didi Goldenhar**
Senior Consultant
Advancing Women Professionals
and the Jewish Community

**Marty Linsky**
Co-founder and Principal
Cambridge Leadership Associates

www.advancingwomen.org

www.cambridge-leadership.com

Copyright © 2008 by
Advancing Women Professionals
and the Jewish Community, and
Cambridge Leadership Associates

First edition 2008

Creative Direction by
Hillary Leone, Cabengo LLC

Graphic Design by
Beverly Joel, pulp, ink.

Printing by
Print Craft, Inc.,
St. Paul, Minnesota

We would like to thank Barbara and Eric Dobkin of the Dobkin Family Foundation, AWP's wonderful philanthropic partners who have given generously of their wisdom and funding. We are deeply grateful to Terry Meyerhoff Rubenstein and the Lyn P. Meyerhoff Foundation, Sally Gottesman, and Froma Benerofe for their outstanding commitment to supporting AWP's work over many years. We are also very fortunate to receive funding from the Richard and Rhoda Goldman Fund. Slingshot's recognition of AWP's work has been extremely valuable.

AWP's Board of Directors, Cindy Chazan, Barbara Dobkin, Judith Stern Peck, and Audrey Weiner always provide strategic and intelligent guidance, and we appreciate their excellent counsel. AWP has also benefited tremendously from the thoughtful involvement of its advisors: David Altshuler, Lotte Bailyn, Audra P. Berg, Steven M. Cohen, Joyce K. Fletcher, Ruth Flicker, Sherry Israel, Jonathan Jacoby, Meryle Mahrer Kaplan, Shaul Kelner, Eve Landau, Hillary Leone, Nessa Rapaport, Jacob Solomon, Nancy Schwartz Sternoff, Virginia Valian, and Marie Wilson. Our appreciation to Melanie Lewis, AWP's executive assistant, and to Sandra Gary, who has been a terrific editorial assistant and a loyal colleague.

And we would like to thank Marty's colleagues at CLA, particularly Elizabeth Nill, Jeff McEwen, and Alexander Grashow, who believed in the purpose of this project and encouraged us to see it through, no matter how many hours it consumed.

This book was strengthened by the insightful critiques of: Robyn Champion, Steven M. Cohen, Sharna Goldseker, Jill Herman, Ilana Kurshan, Morlie Levin, and Sivanie Shiran.

You have all been co-creators in this effort to bring greater equity and excellence in Jewish life.

We dedicate *Leveling the Playing Field* to the memory of Lisa Goldberg. Her extraordinary life, and her groundbreaking work as president of The Charles H. Revson Foundation, exemplified Lisa's profound commitment to women, leadership, democracy, and change.

# Contents

# Contents

# PREFACE

# Who We Are

This guidebook results from a partnership between two organizations – **Advancing Women Professionals and the Jewish Community** and **Cambridge Leadership Associates**. Our hope is that, through this fruitful collaboration, we are modeling some of the behaviors that we suggest in the pages that follow.

### ADVANCING WOMEN PROFESSIONALS (AWP)

The mission of Advancing Women Professionals and the Jewish Community (AWP) is to advance women into leadership in Jewish life; stimulate Jewish organizations to become productive, equitable, and vibrant environments; and promote policies that support work-life integration and new models of leadership.

Women represent a majority of the Jewish communal workforce, yet few have risen to top positions. Many talented women find they cannot reach their full potential in the Jewish community. The community, in turn, is diminished by the talent drain that results when women leave the Jewish professional field – or choose not to enter in the first place.

AWP, a national nonprofit organization, seeks to leverage the talents of women on behalf of the Jewish community and to act as a catalyst for change. AWP has found that identifying the systemic barriers that prevent women from advancing, leads to discovering the challenges that exist for everyone in the workplace – women and men, professionals and volunteers. Through research, pilot projects, advocacy, and publications, AWP is removing barriers and helping Jewish organizations establish policies and practices that expand opportunities for everyone.

## CAMBRIDGE LEADERSHIP ASSOCIATES (CLA)

Cambridge Leadership Associates (CLA) is a consulting practice built around the principles of Adaptive Leadership™ and committed to working with individuals and organizations to develop the leadership capacity to move forward and reach their most important goals.

Adaptive Leadership is an approach that differentiates between technical problems, which, although they may be complicated, have known solutions, and adaptive challenges, the deep-seated, intractable issues for which there are no easy answers. Adaptive challenges are the ones that divide loyalties, block progress, and require that we change hearts, minds, and behaviors in order to make progress.

CLA is both realistic and optimistic, believing that true leadership is difficult to practice, but that behaviors can be learned, a shared language and set of understandings achieved, and stalemates and deadlocks overcome, so that change can be accelerated. CLA helps individuals learn to lead effectively within the context of their organizations by practicing Adaptive Leadership™ and dealing directly with the value conflicts, personal and system dynamics, resistance, and turmoil that are inevitable in achieving meaningful change.

This book also emerges from the collaboration between three of us as coauthors – Shifra, Didi, and Marty. A few words of introduction may be in order about how each of us comes to this book:

Shifra, who founded AWP, brings decades of experience in progressive social change to this work. She has been on the forefront as a speaker and writer, both as a nonprofit professional CEO and as executive vice president for one of New York City's largest privately-owned real estate firms. In more recent times, her belief in a more vital Jewish community inspired her to create AWP as well as her own consulting firm, which specializes in advocacy and change initiatives. It is really because of Shifra's passion and purpose that we come to this project.

Didi is a longtime colleague and friend of Shifra's, going back more than twenty-five years. In addition to her career as a consultant to a wide range of organizations, Didi brings her background in theater and poetry to this book. While this may seem counter-intuitive to the subject matter, we benefited from her writer's ear and editor's sense of narrative, chapter by chapter.

Marty came into this project as a result of meeting Shifra and pursuing his interest in the Jewish community and in women's leadership; we also suspect that he was enthusiastic about joining a project that would champion the underdog. Marty's extensive and varied background in media and politics, as well as his experience as a consultant and teacher around Adaptive Leadership, made him a welcome writing and thinking partner.

We all came to this project at different stages of parenthood: Marty with his children, Alison, Sam, and Max, launched into adulthood; Didi's son, Luc, off to college, and Shifra, a late-in-life mother of two younger children, Emma and Coby. We know that these varied experiences influenced our thinking about how to navigate life and work.

Over the past three years, we have worked together – digging into ideas, trading drafts, questioning each other's assumptions and occasionally arguing with great zest over big and small issues while working our way through take-out soups and salads. We have learned together, pushed each other, tried to model behavior that we advocate, and, in this book, finally come to what we hope is a useful meeting of the minds.

# INTRODUCTION

# The Challenge:
# Taking on a Gender Equity Initiative
# in Your Organization

This guidebook is about how to create a particular kind of organizational change in a particular kind of organization – *advancing women and creating gender equity in Jewish organizations.*

If you believe that gender equity is vital to the health of Jewish communities and want to turn your beliefs into productive action, then this guidebook is for you.

The strategies and tools in this guidebook will be relevant wherever you are positioned in your organization. The goals and tactics may vary depending on your formal and informal roles, but the opportunity for exercising leadership on gender equity is available to you whether you are sitting in the corner office or just getting started in your career.

You can make a difference whether you are a:

- CEO or member of the senior management team;
- Middle manager;
- Young professional early in your career;
- Volunteer leader who contributes time, expertise, and money; or
- Volunteer leader whose primary commitment is as a donor.

## Our Purpose and Objectives

From the beginning, our work on this guidebook has been motivated by three objectives:

- To provide a resource guide to the strategic options and tactical tools for a gender equity initiative that is right for you and for your organization;
- To share our learning from gender equity initiatives in Jewish communal organizations and other fields; and
- To give you a deeper understanding of why leading organizational change is difficult and how you can minimize the risks and maximize your chances of success.

## Making the Case: Our Three Core Assumptions

To begin, we think it's a good idea to state our core assumptions, drawn from our own research and experience.

- **Gender inequity is embedded in Jewish organizational life.**
- **Gender equity is vital to the health of Jewish communal organizations.**
- **Creating gender equity will improve overall workplace effectiveness.**

### GENDER INEQUITY IS EMBEDDED IN JEWISH ORGANIZATIONAL LIFE

Many research studies and articles have documented the persistence of gender inequity in the Jewish communal sector:

A 2002 article in the *Journal of Jewish Communal Service* scanned the leadership of every national Jewish organization. The article noted that male CEOs led *all but one* of the major agencies and denomination-specific religious organizations (Bronznick 2002).

A study of forty-eight major Jewish organizations found that out of 2,315 board members, only 25% were women. Moreover, only five organizations were headed by a female president or copresident, and 53% had no women in their five highest salaried positions (Horowitz, Beck, and Kadushin 1997).

Eight years later, another study explored the impact of gender on philanthropic careers. The alumni of the **Wexner Heritage Program** for Jewish volunteer leaders were surveyed in 2005 about leadership positions held in the past five years. Male and female alumni were almost equally represented at the level of committee chairperson. However, at the level of board member or board president, women were underrepresented (Chertok, Saxe, et al. 2005).

**AWP and United Jewish Communities (UJC)** released a comprehensive study in 2004 that documented gender inequity throughout the Jewish federation system. The report presented evidence and analysis of the factors that contribute to the "leaky pipeline" for women professionals in the system (Cohen, Bronznick, et al. 2004).

The **AWP-UJC Gender Equity Project** has released annual reports on job positions in the federation system, starting in 2004. These

IN THE JEWISH WORLD
## AWP-UJC Report: Key Factors in the Leaky Pipeline

- The executive search process relies on a largely male network for referral and recruitment of candidates.

- In fundraising, the potential of women to solicit major gifts was questioned despite the success of women in senior fundraising positions and despite philanthropic trends that suggest greater receptivity to women from younger donors.

- Leadership style is viewed differently depending on gender. For example, an "aggressive" style is often seen as positive and necessary for men but as a negative attribute in women.

- Work-life balance and challenges of relocation impede women's advancement significantly. While these issues also affect men, they have more of a negative impact on women.

- Weaknesses in human resource development throughout the federation system affect women disproportionately.

- Gender-based assumptions abound in the system, suggesting the need for education around gender issues.

reports show that women make up the vast majority of professionals in Jewish federations. In fact, women's representation in the senior ranks has been growing over the last three years; as of 2006, women constitute the majority of professionals holding senior management positions other than chief executive officer.

However, notwithstanding these encouraging gains, Professor Steven M. Cohen notes in the conclusion to his 2006 report, "Women are absent, or nearly absent, from the most influential, prestigious and best-compensated jobs in the system: the executives of large and large-intermediate communities. The evidence points to no change in this category of the 40 or so top jobs in the system."

## Percentage of Female Chief Executives at Jewish Federations

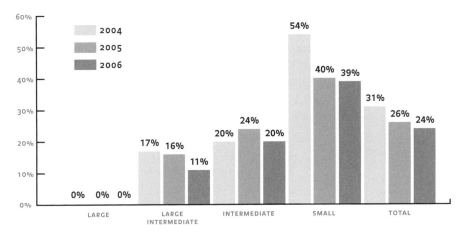

Several recent studies underscore the **gender gap in salary** in the Jewish communal sector:

In the 2002 study of **Jewish Community Centers**, men serving as executive director and assistant director earned an average of nearly $19,000 more than women serving in the same positions (Schor and Cohen 2002).

A 2004 study of **Conservative rabbis** showed that male rabbis earn more than their female counterparts, whether measured in terms of annual income or total compensation package – even after controlling for full- or part-time work and size of congregation. The salary gap ranged from $10,000 to $27,000 (Cohen and Schor 2004).

In 2006, the CMJS and Fisher Bernstein Institute for Jewish Philanthropy and Leadership released a six-community study of the Jewish sector workforce which observed, "Although women are a majority of Jewish sector workers, advantages continue to flow to men." The study presented evidence of gender-related disparities in compensation, "on the order of tens of thousands of dollars," regardless of age, organizational tenure, graduate training, supervisory responsibilities, and membership on the senior management team (Kelner, Rabkin, et al. 2005).

## GENDER EQUITY IS VITAL TO THE HEALTH OF JEWISH COMMUNAL ORGANIZATIONS

This is not a question of ideology, but of logic. Meritocracies, where the most capable people are hired and promoted, are broadly representative of the community from which they draw. The Jewish communal field is staffed predominantly by women, yet the majority of CEO positions are occupied by men. An organization with overwhelmingly male leadership, despite a majority of female staff, is not likely to be operating as a meritocracy and therefore is not taking full advantage of its talent pool.

We know that diversity in leadership contributes to an organization's effectiveness – *externally*, by connecting to more segments of the community and *internally*, by generating a broader set of perspectives and ideas.

Gender equity also contributes to the bottom line. When organizations are cultivating talent at every level, and people feel they are fulfilling their potential, productivity increases and staff turnover decreases. Every CEO knows that high turnover translates into higher recruitment and training costs; these transitions also are expensive in terms of staff morale.

Catalyst, the leading organization for advancing women in business, has studied the link between gender diversity in leadership and corporate performance. Its 2004 report of more than 350 Fortune 500 companies found that those with the highest representation of women on top management teams had performed better financially than companies with the lowest women's representation, as measured by return on equity (ROE) and total return to share-holders (TRS) (Catalyst 2004).

CREATING GENDER EQUITY WILL IMPROVE
OVERALL WORKPLACE EFFECTIVENESS

The link between advancing women and strengthening workplace performance is at the core of Lotte Bailyn and Joyce Fletcher's groundbreaking work at M.I.T. and Simmons School of Management. Their research demonstrates that uncovering assumptions in the workplaces – about what is valued, who is seen as competent, and how professional commitment is assessed – also reveals the elements that affect women's advancement. These scholar-practitioners suggest that the best way to achieve gender equity is through a *dual agenda* that connects equity and effectiveness. First, identify the factors that make it hard for women to advance. Second, identify the values, behaviors, and policies that can be changed to benefit women *and* the work.

Here's an example:

Bailyn and her team brought their method of Collaborative Interactive Action Research (CIAR) to an international aid agency. They discovered that the agency rewarded staff members who traveled widely in the field, launching new projects. These professionals were valued as competent and successful. Staff members in the home office, who provided support and analysis for existing programs, were overlooked. As it turned out, most of the project "launchers" were male as many of the women could not manage the frequent travel required for new projects. Women were relegated to the invisible sustainer roles.

Working with the CIAR researchers, the agency's leadership re-evaluated their assumptions about organizational success. First, they conceded that frequent travel to the field led to some negative consequences since grantees tended to become overly dependent on program officers. Second, they acknowledged that their emphasis on new projects reduced their capacity to sustain ongoing projects, since the limited staff in the home office was responsible for an ever-increasing portfolio.

As a result of the CIAR process, these agency leaders made

significant changes. They balanced the portfolio of new and ongoing projects. Travel for new projects was curtailed. With fewer travel assignments, more women could participate in field projects. Finally, the value system for staff recognition and rewards was revised, so that ongoing projects were elevated to comparable status with the launch of new projects. Women benefited from these changes, and the agency's work improved overall.

## Why is a Guidebook Needed?

If we know the problems around gender equity in Jewish organizational life, and we know some of the solutions, then why is a guidebook needed?

### MOVING AN ORGANIZATION FROM GENDER INEQUITY TO GENDER EQUITY IS A DEEP CHANGE – AN ADAPTIVE CHALLENGE RATHER THAN A TECHNICAL PROBLEM

The single biggest mistake people make in exercising leadership is treating *adaptive challenges* as if they were *technical problems.*

*Technical problems* live above the neck: they are susceptible to a good argument or to someone's expertise. *Adaptive challenges* live between the neck and the navel: they are about values and beliefs, ways of being, and sense of self.

*Adaptive challenges* are not about logic. They are about the experience of loss – the loss of what is familiar and comfortable, including expectations and rewards, and the loss of what people think of as the values that guide their everyday decisions.

Tampering with people's values is a different kind of work than influencing their logic. That's why leading deep organizational change is so difficult. And, while we may have a vision of what gender equity looks like, we have no guarantees about what the change will look like along the way, or how long the journey will take. Deep organizational change may take from seven to ten years. So, much of the difficulty of adaptive challenge is about tolerating the losses and ambiguous terrain that lie between the status quo and the Promised Land.

Here are a couple of examples that illustrate the difference between technical problems and adaptive challenges:

You go to your doctor with a broken finger. A broken finger is a complex *technical problem* that may require a cast, a splint, and some extra care in your daily activities. But many doctors can attend to the problem of a broken finger.

But what if you have high cholesterol? That's a different kind of problem. Your doctor can prescribe medication that may help. But she can't take your pills for you, and, more important, she can't stop eating chocolate ice cream for you or get up an hour earlier to exercise for you. Her expertise is useful, but the *adaptive challenge* lies within you. You will have to give up something you love – chocolate ice cream or that extra hour in bed – in favor of your health.

Here's an illustration from the Jewish world:

Your agency does not have a kosher kitchen. But when the organization hires its first Orthodox Jew, he asks if the kitchen can be koshered and kept kosher. Some staff members embrace the idea; others say that this is a major imposition. The CEO supports the change, saying that a Jewish organization should respect its most observant member. New dishes and utensils are purchased, and the appliances are blow-torched. That speaks to the *technical problem*.

Two months later, the meat and milk dishes still get mixed up despite elaborate systems to label everything. The *technical problem* has been solved, but the nonkosher staff members are resisting the *adaptive challenge*. They value their own religious choices; for them, a kosher kitchen at work means giving up individual freedoms, like bringing leftovers from home or ordering from the local pizzeria.

Organizations typically try to address adaptive challenges as technical problems. Individuals and groups will almost always try to interpret issues as technical, individual, and win-win, rather than adaptive and systemic. That way, no one has to endure any losses or deal with conflict.

Advancing gender equity in Jewish organizational life is an adaptive challenge because it will expose the gap between the espoused values of the agency, as expressed by the people at the top, and the real norms, as embodied by day-to-day behaviors. Part of your role will be to keep the adaptive change central – with all its disturbing implications – while the pressure is on to come up with short-term, technical Band-Aids that allow you to avoid dealing with the deeper issues.

Most adaptive challenges involve some technical aspects. Sometimes a Band-Aid approach is the only way to start the change process. Sometimes a modest, more technical idea can test the waters, and you can incorporate this idea into a larger, more ambitious strategy. But be forewarned: since most organizations gravitate toward technical fixes, you will have to evaluate at each step along the way whether a proposed technical fix is a step toward an adaptive change or a diversion away from it.

## LEADING DEEP ORGANIZATIONAL CHANGE, SUCH AS A GENDER EQUITY INITIATIVE, IS DIFFICULT WORK

If you embrace this challenge, be prepared for the difficulty ahead.

There is an idea that people do not like change. Wrong. Winning the lottery will certainly change your life, but no one gives away a winning lottery ticket.

People resist significant change when they experience it as a threat or as a potential loss, no matter how good they think it will be for them.

Resistance to gender equity will surface in all the familiar arguments – that there are no qualified women for high-level jobs; that women aren't good fundraisers; that women choose family before work; that the statistics don't prove anything; that raising gender issues will lead to lawsuits or embarrassing stories in the media; or that the issue is effectiveness, not gender equity.

Be prepared for this resistance since it is likely to appear in both direct and indirect forms. When an organization makes a commitment to gender equity, people who benefit from the current system may feel threatened. Men who have been waiting for their chance at the brass ring – and doing everything expected of them along the way – may feel cheated if the rules of engagement change. The same may be true for women who have adapted to the male-dominated culture by already making significant compromises in their personal or professional lives in order to succeed.

In the face of resistance, you and your colleagues will need to exercise consistent leadership. People typically avoid leadership because it means putting themselves out there – taking risks and making people uncomfortable. That's why exercising leadership requires both skill and courage. Which brings us to our guidebook.

## How to Use This Guidebook

When you embark on any new adventure – whether a trip to a far-flung country or a gender equity initiative – a guidebook can spark your imagination and help you anticipate the unexpected. In the same way, we include lessons from our own work at AWP and CLA, as well as reflections and stories from people throughout the Jewish world who have led organizational change. Their practical smarts, profound wisdom, and good humor will give you an extra measure of good sense and inspiration as you begin to make your way.

This guidebook unfolds in three parts:

In **Part I: The Adaptive Challenge**, we explore the reasons gender inequity is so prevalent throughout Jewish organizational life, and we introduce the behaviors and techniques that will help you and your colleagues achieve deep organizational change.

In **Part II: The Work Ahead**, we describe a three-step process for organizational change: Assessment, Intervention, and Monitoring and Accountability.

In **Part III: Strategies for Change**, we concentrate on the areas where you and your colleagues might focus your efforts: Expanding Opportunities for Advancement, Increasing Equality, and Improving the Quality of Life and Work.

We encourage you to approach this guide in your own fashion. You might want to read it cover-to-cover, absorbing the theory before moving into the work itself. Or you may want to go directly to the Strategies section, to read about a particular change effort that you have in mind.

Regardless of your approach, you will find theory linked to practice throughout this guidebook, to help you successfully apply this work on the ground. You also can download practical tools and resources from AWP's Web site: www.advancingwomen.org.

We have great aspirations for this work, for this guidebook, and for you. We hope that what we offer in these pages will sustain your commitment, reinforce your courage, and strengthen your capacity to create real change.

# PART I

# The Adaptive Challenge

Systems are what they are for a reason. It's not serendipitous. The arrangements, behaviors, and rules – written and unwritten – serve real goals and objectives or else they would have been changed.

This is as true for gender inequity in Jewish organizations as it is for income inequality in America. No one says that they favor the gap between rich and poor. But many people behave as though they want these inequities to continue. Why? Because other values, purposes, and loyalties are more important to them. If gender equity or income inequality is far down on the list of issues that you or others care about, these may as well be off the list entirely.

For individuals and groups within organizations, the unwillingness to choose among competing, and dearly held, values creates an immunity to change.

Here's one example of how *competing values* operate within the Jewish federation system:

The CEOs of the twenty largest federations meet regularly as a group, including an annual retreat. It is widely understood that these CEOs exert enormous influence on the policies and programs of the entire Federation system.

From the perspective of these CEOs, there is good reason to confine these meetings to the twenty largest federations. These executives raise the most money and need a forum to discuss the unique issues that derive from their size and the Jewish communities that they represent.

However, the consequence of honoring that value – limiting participation to large-city CEOs – means that only one woman professional (the executive leader of United Israel Appeal in Canada) currently occupies a seat at that very powerful table. Women's voices are virtually absent from these meetings. Is it any surprise that, for this group, the issue of gender equity is of low priority?

These executives do not think of themselves as being opposed to gender equity, nor do they believe that they are doing anything wrong. From where they sit, this meeting makes sense. Why disturb a system that has elevated them to senior authority?

## Behind the Curve in the Jewish Community

We know that the gender gap exists in almost every line of work. The media regularly chronicles the difficulties faced by women in most professions. Even so, the Jewish community lags far behind the curve. There are fewer women at the high echelons in the Jewish communal arena than in comparable organizations in academia, philanthropy, and the secular nonprofit sector.

Moreover, the Jewish community is one of the few sectors that have *not* made serious efforts to advance gender equity. Strategies to address gender inequities have been pursued in law, medicine, business, politics, and academia; while women are still underrepresented at the upper ranks of these fields, they have made quantifiable gains. Jewish women certainly have distinguished themselves in every arena – from universities to foundations and from the Senate floor to the

Supreme Court. By contrast, the Jewish community has invested very little to expand opportunities for women.

What particular aspects of our community might account for this difference? From our experience, there are several *cultural attitudes* that rank high in Jewish organizational life, but which also inhibit gender equity. Here's our list. As you read, think about which ones apply to your situation:

**We're one big Jewish family.** The family atmosphere that permeates Jewish organizational life allows gender stereotypes to flourish. Young women predominate at the entry level and in the middle ranks. Older men congregate at the top. This organizational design, underscored by the influence of older male lay leaders, creates a family pattern in which "good daughters" find it hard to demand positions of power.

**You can't fix what you can't see.** All nonprofit organizations cultivate donors and board members. In Jewish communal life, however, the unique collaboration between volunteers and staff is valued more than individual professional achievement. The complexity of this volunteer-professional relationship makes it harder to establish and recognize objective standards of performance.

**This is my job *and* my Jewish life.** Communal professionals view their work as a vehicle for pursuing their Jewish identity. Commitment to the Jewish people feels ideologically sound and personally fulfilling. However, this commitment sometimes influences women to set aside their own needs and aspirations. For many women, this translates into a willingness to live with the salary gender gap or other types of discrimination.

**We are saving the world.** Most Jewish organizations focus on rescue and renewal. We save others by fundraising, social action, and fighting anti-Semitism. We build community and Jewish identity, here at home and around the world. With such noble and altruistic aims, the internal work of human resource development is seen as a distraction that pulls us away from our mission-driven activities.

**Shush. Don't tell the donors.** The Jewish fear of "airing dirty laundry in public" makes it risky to raise the issue of gender bias. Our organizations are characterized by boosterism – all our messages must be framed as successes, e.g., "The campaign is on the upswing!" Donors are shielded from internal problems, and in this environment, admitting the presence of gender bias is seen as unproductive.

What *beliefs* influence the way that women are treated in Jewish organizations? What are the *realities* that challenge these beliefs?

The way women are treated in Jewish organizations satisfies other competing, but highly cherished, values. Here are some examples of gender-related *beliefs* in the Jewish community and the *realities* that contradict them:

**The Stepping-Stone Belief:** Jewish organizations are great training grounds for women. Look at how many young, talented women are going into the communal field.
**Reality:** Young, talented, and committed Jewish women start their careers in communal organizations, accepting low-paying jobs and doing great work. However, within several years, frustrated by the lack of career development and the reality of the glass ceiling, many of these young women take their career aspirations elsewhere. They are then replaced by other talented, committed young professionals. This revolving door sustains the status quo for those senior professionals who do not want their job security challenged.

**The All-in-Good-Time Belief:** We have a lot of women working in Jewish organizations. Over time, some of them will reach the top.
**Reality:** The belief that women's leadership will evolve naturally over time satisfies many leaders – both professionals and volunteers – who would prefer that this shift take place *after their tenure*. They fear that the feminization of the Jewish communal field will lead to a decline in its prestige and effectiveness. As a result, many leaders erect, consciously and unconsciously, many barriers against high-potential women.

**The Round-the-Clock Belief:** Jewish organizations require 24/7 or 24/6 commitment from CEOs and senior leaders. Women won't put their professional lives ahead of their families.
**Reality:** Work-life balance is becoming a primary factor in job choice and job satisfaction in the Jewish world and in the larger society. Many young people – women and men – are no longer willing to devote

24/7 to their professional lives. Smart companies and organizations are learning how to accommodate a range of career aspirations in order to gain competitive advantage in talent recruitment and retention. But many Jewish organization leaders are reluctant to consider that their own sacrifices, which they accepted as the price of leadership, will not be embraced by the next generation.

Finally, there is the persistent belief held by some male communal leaders that women lack the fundraising clout needed in chief executive positions. We have heard this articulated in research interviews and informally in one-on-one meetings. *Let's put this myth to rest.* Throughout the communal arena, women professionals are succeeding in top fundraising posts. Outside the Jewish world, women now lead 23% of universities in the United States, in positions that demand extraordinary fundraising talent. The fact that women can succeed in presidential posts, including four in the Ivy League, should make it abundantly clear: women can be highly effective fundraisers for large nonprofit institutions.

Letting go of these beliefs – seeing them as *assumptions* rather than truths – is an important step forward in the process of change.

## Adaptive Change: The Leadership Toolkit

Given the cultural attitudes and beliefs that keep the Jewish community behind the curve, what kinds of behaviors will change them? What will you and your colleagues have to do differently in order to exercise leadership in this area?

Leading adaptive change is about getting people to address the gap between their espoused values and the current reality. You will need to proceed in a different way than you would for a technical problem that can be solved by logic.

So here is our basic **Leadership Toolkit** – an overview of six qualities and behaviors that we believe are essential for leading adaptive change. We will come back to these in more detail in the next chapter – "The Work Ahead" – as you begin to map out your gender equity effort.

## GET ON THE BALCONY

Perhaps the most important skill in leading adaptive change is *getting on the balcony*, or taking a distanced view, to assess what is really going on, even when you're also on the dance floor, getting caught up in the action. Getting on the balcony is especially important early on, when you're diagnosing your organization.

When you're on the balcony, you ask questions and look for clues: What's about to happen that may affect your organization and/or your change effort? What's going on elsewhere in your Jewish community? What connections or adjustments should you make, based on what's happening inside your organization, in the wider Jewish community, in the broader nonprofit community, or in the world at large?

## THINK POLITICALLY
## (IT'S ALL ABOUT RELATIONSHIPS)

Being right about the merits of gender equity is not enough for *adaptive change*. You need to articulate the case in a persuasive way, but if all change required was a compelling argument, gender equity would be the norm and there would be no need for this guidebook. You are taking on this initiative because of the *gap* between what people say they believe – what the system *says* it stands for – and the *actual behaviors*.

Thinking politically means focusing on relationships and their underlying influence. Who has the most to gain if your initiative is successful? Who has the most to lose? Who are your potential allies, even if their reasons differ from yours? Who are the people who *say* they are with you, but who do not have the courage to step out publicly? What inspiration or incentives would it take to get these people to take the leap?

Adaptive change is all about relationships. To move from diagnosis to intervention will call upon all your relationship-building skills and your awareness of organizational dynamics. Here are some ideas for managing the relationships and alliances that will be necessary to move your initiative forward:

**Resist the urge to go it alone.** Change processes often fail when people try to go it alone. This seems obvious. But people do end up alone (and vulnerable) on the barricades for several reasons. People who are uncomfortable with change would rather marginalize or isolate the

**Donna M. Rosenthal**, executive vice chairman of CLAL, the National Jewish Center for Learning and Leadership:

You have to build all kinds of alliances. In the beginning I thought I had to deal with all the issues all by myself. What I learned was to go out and talk to others, not only to see where we all were, but to build a supportive cadre. That was a learning process. I'm a social worker, and I actually learned that in school. But in my own work, I didn't initially apply it to myself. Women often think they're alone. They're not alone. Even if you are the only woman in the environment, there are others thinking in the same way, whatever the situation. You're really not alone in almost anything you do.

change agent. Even your allies and friends will prefer that *you* test the ice before they join you. Remember, the passion and commitment that moves you to action may also push you farther out in front than you need to be, especially if you're seen as caring about gender equity at the expense of the organization or your professional responsibilities.

**Tailor your approach.** Each of us comes to this work with competencies and deficits. Tailoring your approach means finding people who possess skills that you're missing or who bring the strengths that compensate for your vulnerabilities.

Take advantage of the water cooler or lunchtime to sound people out about their attitudes. Be curious. Don't make speeches. Listen to what people say at meetings. Who is open to new ideas? Who seems to embrace innovation? Be attentive to opportunities. For example, listen to the way that people talk about their professional aspirations and disappointments or about the stresses in their personal lives.

Tailor your approach to suit each person (just as in fundraising). Who will respond to an e-mail for an informal meeting after work? Who needs a more careful invitation? Who requires the help of an intermediary, a colleague or friend who will make the first introduction?

**Cultivate volunteer-professional partnerships.** Thinking politically means appreciating the central role of the volunteer-professional relationship in Jewish communal life. Volunteer leaders wield tremendous influence in setting agendas, mapping strategy, allocating resources, and building support from their peers.

Given these influential partnerships, it follows that, for a gender equity change initiative, you need to engage your volunteer or professional counterparts. Give careful thought to these relationships. Your challenge is to assess other people's perspectives, so that you have a realistic sense of what you can expect them to do on behalf of this initiative.

**Look for unlikely allies.** Coalitions are more effective when they go beyond the usual suspects. Unlikely allies might include, for example, retired professional women who bring credibility from their many years of service and who would like to make the journey less stressful for their successors; older men in the volunteer or professional ranks who have daughters trying to balance career and family, and enlightened philanthropists who support women's causes in their non-Jewish civic lives.

**Create a circle of outside advisors.** In addition to a coalition of internal allies, consider engaging informal outside advisors; for example, people who offer expertise from their research, people from other fields who live in your community and have led similar initiatives, or people who study organizational change. This is a group you can approach to ask questions and test strategic ideas.

From the beginning, AWP has relied on a brain trust of leaders and scholars from the Jewish community, academics renowned for their research on gender and the workplace, executive recruiters, consultants from Catalyst, and colleagues from Ma'yan and the White House Project. At the start, we convened these colleagues as an informal design team; since then, we have approached them individually and as a group to help assess progress, make midcourse corrections, and plan next steps.

### ORCHESTRATE THE CONFLICT

To get on the agenda, you need to stimulate conversation about gender equity. To do so, you will position yourself, not as the advocate, but as the *facilitator* of uncomfortable conversations about the importance of gender equity and what the organization might have to sacrifice on its behalf.

Your organization will probably try to reduce the tension, but you need to keep the issue alive. That means raising the heat high enough so that people face up to the tension and work it through.

For example, when AWP and UJC published and distributed their research on gender bias in the federation system, the intention was to raise the heat. The report revealed, through scores of anonymous quotes from volunteer and professional leaders, the overt and widespread sexism in the system. Jewish newspapers nationwide gave front-page placement to the story. The report was sent to thousands of Jewish professionals and volunteers.

At the same time, AWP *orchestrated the conflict*. Instead of presenting specific prescriptions for change, AWP facilitated a series of group conversations – first with federation CEOs, then with UJC's Board of Trustees, and finally with more than 130 professionals from UJC. The goal was to elicit candid reactions to the report and to collect ideas about next steps from supporters and naysayers. As a result, a diverse group of professionals and volunteers in the federation system has been involved in thinking through the challenges of achieving gender equity and coming up with meaningful solutions.

## AWP Advisors

Catalyst is the leading resource and advisory organization working with businesses and the professions to build inclusive environments and expand opportunities for women in the workplace. www.catalyst.org.

The Center for Gender in Organizations (CGO) at Simmons School of Management analyzes the influence of gender in workplace practices and culture. CGO's work focuses on a dual agenda – a systemic linking of equity and effectiveness that enables both women and men to be productive contributors. www.simmons.edu/som/cgo.

Gender Equity Project (GEP) at Hunter College – leads the way in demolishing the glass ceiling for academic women scientists. www.hunter.cuny.edu/genderequity.

Ma'yan: The Jewish Women's Project of the JCC in Manhattan acts as a catalyst for change through its development of resources, rituals, publications, and leadership programs for women and girls in the Jewish community. www.mayan.org.

The White House Project is a nonpartisan organization that aims to make American institutions, business, and government truly inclusive – up to the U.S. presidency – by filling the leadership pipeline with a richly diverse, critical mass of women. www.thewhitehouseproject.org.

## HOLD STEADY

People will find creative ways to get you to back off from your purpose. You need to hold steady. Resistance is a sign that you are onto something. The resistance is not personal to you, even if it is framed that way.

You need to keep the issue in front of the group and push the work back to them, so that they struggle with their choices, act experimentally, pursue an intervention, and see what happens. And you need to be flexible enough to apply what you learn along the way, making corrections as the project moves forward.

## TAKE THE HEAT

Take the heat, but don't take it personally. Bullies know that many people back away when the heat – the conflict – begins to intensify. Working on your own capacity to absorb heat, put criticism in context, and be a lightning rod for other people's anxieties is no different from training any other skill or muscle. If you prepare yourself, when an issue arises, you'll be less apt to react emotionally in a way that undermines your purpose and serves the interests of those who'd like to see your initiative fail.

By taking on a gender equity initiative, you may be putting your role in jeopardy on behalf of a value that you care about. You may be warned about taking on an issue that is beyond your scope of authority. For example, if you are a young woman professional, you will be seen as self-interested. If you are a middle manager, you may be perceived as stirring up trouble. If you are a CEO, you will be accused of diverting the organization from its noble purposes. If you are a significant donor who starts talking about tying your donations to improving gender equity, you will destabilize relationships with long-time associates and friends. You may be marginalized so that other people don't have to face the issue of gender equity that you represent.

**Judy Yudof**, honorary international president of the United Synagogue of Conservative Judaism, spoke about what happened after she raised the issue of whether the Movement's Law Committee should reconsider its position on homosexuality:

It catapulted me in a way I could not have imagined. I never imagined that I would be called reckless by the highest voices in our Movement. I have had to stand up to that. You find out what it's like to be at the end of a limb where there is a buzz saw going. You do get the wonderful occasional letter that makes it all worthwhile. But it's been very challenging. You have to remember what your heart of hearts tells you is the right thing to do, which isn't necessarily the easy thing to do. Just don't lose sight of the target.

## ANCHOR YOURSELF

Leading deep organizational change can be challenging, stressful, and surprisingly lonely work. You may find yourself becoming vulnerable to many pressures – those that you put on yourself, and those that others transfer to you. Take care of yourself:

**Find confidantes.** You need one or more confidantes. A confidante doesn't care as much about your initiative as she does about you. You can pour your heart out to this person, and it will have no consequences other than eliciting useful feedback. It is tempting but unwise to seek confidantes in your own organization or on the team you've assembled to move the initiative. These people have other interests and loyalties. A confidante is a person whose first loyalty is to you.

**Create sanctuary.** You need sanctuary, regular time to recover, to relax, and most important, to restore your perspective and rekindle your sense of humor. The work of gender equity is very important, but it does not define all that you are, and the survival of the world is not at stake. The roller-coaster ride of advancing Jewish women professionals is the stuff of sitcoms and novels. Try to stand back and enjoy the journey from time to time.

**Remember your purpose.** Sometimes, in the midst of the intensity and especially during a rough patch, you'll need to be reminded why you're doing what you're doing. Going to conferences, surfing the Internet to check out exciting new projects, and especially connecting with like-minded people doing similar work will nourish your sense of purpose. Remember, you and your allies are part of a larger effort within the Jewish community *and* in the larger society: to help women professionals reach their full potential in organizational life.

**Hannah Rosenthal**, executive director of the Chicago Foundation for Women and former executive director of the Jewish Council for Public Affairs (JCPA), has reflected on the conflict that arose from her hiring by male lay leaders:

When I was hired, they said to me, "We're talking our talk and walking our walk and hiring a woman."

I appreciated the symbolism, but I still had an agenda of issues. JCPA was in turmoil in 2002. Many Jewish leaders were trying to close it down. They thought that because I didn't know the system, it would be easy to catch me off-guard. They didn't think I would come up with strategies to get around them. These men were very surprised that I would speak back to them. There were many threats: "We're going to close you down."

I'd say, "Maybe you will," but I kept pushing. The biggest surprise for them is that I was not just symbolic. Their biggest surprise was my competency.

# PART II

# The Work Ahead:
# Diagnosis, Intervention,
# Monitoring
# and Accountability

## DIAGNOSIS

Leading any change initiative begins with a *dual diagnostic*: a clear-eyed assessment of your environment and an equally clear-eyed assessment of yourself. Your plan will flow from the analysis of this dual diagnostic.

### What's the Problem?
### Assessing the Environment

We've learned that research is the first intervention in organizational change. Use data to diagnose current conditions and to decide where to target your change efforts.

Data provides a common fact base – for talking about current conditions and for starting to design change scenarios. Maybe your CEO is confident that his agency is a true meritocracy where women and men are promoted solely on the strength of their skills and achievements. If so, he will not be swayed by the complaints of a few staff members; after all, every office has a few grumbling workers. But an objective account of organizational behavior – with tenure and promotions *by the numbers* – is much harder to ignore.

A common fact base helps to mobilize your allies and enlist others along the way. Some executives or volunteers may be wary of any change effort that seems too "political." But unlike a speech or petition, they may see data as a more objective, neutral instrument. With numbers and patterns in hand, these influential people may be willing to put your report on the agenda of a senior management meeting or the board's nomination committee. However, the data will not speak for itself. Only through interpretation does it become meaningful. For example, data on the gender gap in salary will have greater impact if shown with a five-year trend line. Data also needs to be accompanied by talking points that provide context for the problem and point to possible solutions.

You also can use the data to engage skeptics – especially those professionals and volunteers who've seen previous change efforts launched with good intentions, only to fade away. A public accounting of current conditions is the first step toward *accountability*. Your diagnosis, supported by quantitative and qualitative evidence, will convey the message that this change effort will be different, that progress will be pegged to measurable goals.

The decision to collect previously uncollected data is not neutral nor is it based on idle curiosity. Your decision is based on a hypothesis, and for that reason some people may resist data collection. They do not want to ask questions, the answers to which they may find troublesome. Therefore, as you assess your organization, think about how you will bring potential opponents on board for these first efforts; you probably will need to negotiate with them about the focus of the research as well as the way in which the results will be delivered.

In every field, what matters gets measured. Points, productivity, potholes, profit. We use numbers every day to track progress and drive decisions. In Jewish organizations, we use data all the time to tell us how we're doing. *Is the annual campaign up or down? How many new memberships? Is the number of young couples in our community rising or falling?*

Numbers also tell the story about gender equity. In the corporate sector, law, medicine, and academia – it was the factual data about women in the minority that created the momentum for change. Change is accelerated and gender equity is advanced when managers underscore their stated commitments by counting.

One way to learn about whether your organization offers a level playing field is to *start counting.* Our **Gender Assessment Measurement Tool** (see appendix) offers a list of basic organizational questions, from the number of women in senior management roles to the number of women on the board of directors.

**IN OTHER FIELDS**

## The Impact of Data at M.I.T.

By 1999, the percentage of women in senior faculty posts at the Massachusetts Institute of Technology had remained static at 8% for two decades. Nonetheless, the administration did not accept that gender bias might be a contributing factor.

A group of women professors decided to apply their scientific skills to a study on gender discrimination at M.I.T. They collected comparative data on hiring, promotions, awards, and committee assignments. They even measured the laboratory and office spaces. The resulting evidence was so compelling that then President Charles Vest publicly acknowledged, "I had always believed that contemporary gender discrimination within universities was part reality and part perception... I now understand that reality is by far the greater part of the balance." President Vest subsequently supported a major initiative to address gender issues. And M.I.T is now led by its first woman president, Susan Hockfield.

*Balancing the Equation: Where are Women and Girls in Science, Engineering and Technology?*
Thom, The National Council for Research on Women, 2001.

AWP and United Jewish Communities (UJC) are issuing annual Position Reports that document the percentages of women and men in senior positions in the Federation system. The table below displays position report results for 2004–2006 and illustrates the disparity between men and women in CEO posts.

This data can be used to bolster the *business case* – that given proper resources for training and career development, there is abundant talent to be leveraged for the benefit of the federations.

## Federation Positions by Job Title and Percent Female

| JOB TITLE | 2004 | | 2005 | | 2006 | |
|---|---|---|---|---|---|---|
| | % FEMALE | TOTAL JOBS | % FEMALE | TOTAL JOBS | % FEMALE | TOTAL JOBS |
| Execs, CEOs | 31% | 152 | 26% | 154 | 24% | 155 |
| Associate Execs, COOs | 44% | 34 | 53% | 34 | 52% | 46 |
| Asst Execs | 54% | 37 | 57% | 35 | 62% | 21 |
| CFOs | 50% | 50 | 52% | 52 | 52% | 58 |
| FRD Directors | 33% | 15 | 47% | 17 | 54% | 28 |
| Endowment Directors | 51% | 35 | 55% | 42 | 65% | 43 |
| Campaign Directors | 67% | 45 | 67% | 39 | 71% | 44 |
| Planning Directors | 65% | 31 | 70% | 30 | 69% | 35 |
| Other Professionals | 76% | 1,369 | 77% | 1,510 | 74% | 1,841 |
| Total | 70% | 1,768 | 71% | 1,913 | 70% | 2,271 |

## LOOK FOR PATTERNS

Numbers are important, but to obtain a full picture of the environment, you'll need to collect behavioral data. Look for patterns. Over time, these patterns tell a story about how women are valued and advanced. Again, use our Gender Assessment Measurement Tool to help surface the more subtle factors that contribute to, or take away from, gender equity in your organization. Here are a few questions to get you started:

- What are the patterns for promotion? Women's promotions? Men's promotions?
- How do people get selected for professional opportunities – committees, speaking engagements, special assignments?

- Who represents your organization in public venues?
- What kind of mentoring is going on – formally or informally – for women? For men?
- Over the last few years, who has been credited as the source of good ideas? Whose ideas have been brought to fruition?

## Self-Assessment

Now it's time to focus on you. The next set of questions will guide your thinking about your formal and informal position in the organization, where you are personally in your life and career, your political portfolio, and what resources are available to you.

### WHO ARE YOU, ORGANIZATIONALLY

- What is your *formal position* in the organization?
- What is your *informal position* – your reputation and persona in the organization's internal and external constituencies?
- What are the resources and constraints suggested by your answers to these questions?

### WHERE ARE YOU PERSONALLY, AT THIS STAGE IN YOUR LIFE?

- How well-positioned are you – emotionally, professionally, physically and financially – to move forward on behalf of this issue?
- How much risk does it make sense for you to take?
- What are the resources and constraints suggested by your answers to these questions?

### WHO ARE YOU POLITICALLY?

- What does your own professional network look like?
- Are you identified with particular factions in your organization or in the Jewish community?
- Do you have personal relationships, positive or negative, in surprising places in the community, external or internal?
- What kind of authority do you have? Can you call meetings, control invitation lists, and/or set the agenda of meetings?
- Do you have a special relationship with anyone in a senior authority role? Who has helped you recently? Whom have you helped?

- Do you have a special relationship with anyone in senior authority – professional or volunteer – who can help obtain funding for a gender equity initiative?
- Does your organization offer discretionary funds for professional initiatives around networking, professional development, and career building?
- What in-kind services are available in your organization and community, e.g., meeting space, administrative services, and/or consulting expertise?
- What kind of time can you devote to this effort? Is this strictly extra-curricular or can you request release time to work on this initiative?

## Next Steps: A Deeper Diagnosis

Now that you've completed the first round in the *dual diagnostic*, it's time to deepen the diagnosis – through self-assessment, organizational assessment, and assessment of the external environment.

### GO BACK TO THE SELF-ASSESSMENT

- What strengths and skills do you bring to this initiative?
- What weaknesses and constraints?
- What qualities and roles do you need to complement your own?

With a better sense of your strengths, your weaknesses, and your constraints, you're ready to think about how you will leverage your natural talents and resources *and* how you will engage others to take the lead. This last recommendation may sound counterintuitive. However, being effective often means identifying others who may be better situated – by personality, position, or reputation – to share the leadership with you.

For example, if you're a woman, you may decide to bring in male partners. If you're new to the organization, you need people who have a feel for the history and culture that has led to the current reality. If you're a volunteer, you probably need professional partners and vice versa.

- Who are your organization's key players and groups, both formal (e.g., departmental or board-level) and informal (age, gender, tenure)?
- What is their relationship to the gender equity issue?
- What would their preferred outcome be?
- What are their competing and, perhaps, "higher" loyalties or values?
- What losses might they fear if you are successful?

Here's a chart that uses a hypothetical situation which might be helpful in doing this analysis:

THINKING POLITICALLY STAKEHOLDER MAP
## The Adaptive Issue: Flexible Work Schedules

| PERSON/ GROUP | RELATIONSHIP TO ISSUE | PREFERRED OUTCOMES | COMPETING LOYALTIES & VALUES | POTENTIAL LOSSES |
|---|---|---|---|---|
| MALE EXECUTIVE | No personal stake | Stability | His vision and priorities | Controversy |
| SENIOR WOMEN | Some would benefit; some would not benefit | Unclear | Their own career advancement; not being seen as feminist | Relationships w/executive and board |
| MALE HEAD OF HR | Has working spouse and small children | Change of policy | EVP uninterested; other issues rank higher | Upset boss |

©CLA 2005

Looking at this chart, you can begin to identify who might join you and how to appeal to them. Here are some sample questions:

- As you look at the executive's vision and priorities, what elements might relate to this issue? For example, is the executive interested in cultivating younger couples among his lay leadership?
- As you think about the senior women, who is more secure in her position? Who has been an advocate for women outside the Jewish community, e.g., in local politics?

- How might the head of HR be a valuable support without being in the forefront? For example, does this person have access to HR colleagues elsewhere who have laid the groundwork for flextime or maternity leave?

This two-step diagnosis will begin to show you what a successful coalition might look like – the individuals who should play key roles, the groups or factions who need to be represented, and who might be likely allies. This diagnosis also will help you see beyond the CEO as the only champion of your gender equity initiative. It's important to understand the paradoxical role of the CEO in launching a change effort. The assumption is that change trickles down. However, people at the top are expected to provide stability and order, and those responsibilities cut against leading change. So, it's not surprising that change at the top often needs to be stimulated by people lower on the internal food chain or from outside advocates.

## ASSESS THE EXTERNAL ENVIRONMENT

Thus far you've focused on your organization and on yourself. Now broaden your perspective. What's happening, or about to happen, that may affect your organization or your change effort? What's going on elsewhere in your Jewish community? In your local community? In the headlines? What connections or adjustments should you make, based on what's going on inside your organization, in the Jewish community, in the wider world of nonprofits, or in the world news?

**Shulamit Reinharz**, professor of sociology at Brandeis University and founding director of Brandeis's Women's Studies Research Center:

When an organization is weak, you need to look for one or two very prestigious persons to take the role of director or another elevated title. We used this strategy at the University of Michigan, and it worked beautifully. For building the Women's Studies program, the junior faculty decided who the most prominent women were on campus and asked them to be titular coheads.

When I became an assistant professor at Brandeis and was asked to chair the Women's Studies program, I declined, saying that it was neither good for me (I needed to get tenure) nor for the program – it would not have a powerhouse at its head. When I became a full professor in 1991, I became Chair of the Women's Studies program. I think this strategy works all the time.

# INTERVENTION

Once your coalition begins to take shape, you need to develop a plan. What are the first steps and then the next steps? Who will do the work? What will your role be? As we discussed in the Assessment section, your greatest contribution might be to keep the momentum going and holding people accountable for what they say they will do, rather than being out front. Finally, remember that any strategy that you decide to follow is today's best guess. You'll need to meet frequently with your core group to assess how it is going.

## The Leadership Toolkit, Revisited

As you move your gender equity initiative along, you'll need to keep calling upon the behaviors that we presented in our basic Leadership Toolkit:

- Get on the balcony.
- Think politically (it's all about relationships).
- Orchestrate the conflict.
- Hold steady.
- Take the heat.
- Anchor yourself.

Now we take this Leadership Toolkit to the next level – to give you a preview of the questions and challenges you'll likely face on the ground and how you might be thinking about them:

### HOW PUBLIC DO YOU WANT TO BE?

*Get on the balcony.* As you and your colleagues design a gender equity initiative, consider whether the process should be visible – inside and outside the organization – or whether you should work under the radar.

We usually pursue and recommend a high-profile approach. AWP widely distributed the research findings about bias in the federation system, including broad newspaper coverage. Similarly, when UJC planned the selection process for its Executive Development Program, key allies advocated vigorously – and visibly – for a recruitment goal of 50% women. This was a significant opportunity for UJC to broadcast the message that the federation system was ready to cultivate talented women candidates.

On the other hand, sometimes it's preferable *not* to shine a spotlight on every aspect of your initiative. Several years ago, at a major Jewish organization, a group of women volunteer leaders and senior professionals started meeting to explore how to expand opportunities for women. At first these meetings were announced publicly, but people then decided that it would be preferable for them to take place without fanfare, as informal gatherings where women could experiment with new ways of becoming more visible and influential. Ultimately, with the support and involvement of the CEO and other male board leaders, the women began to rise to positions of prominence. Keeping the "women only" meetings off the radar screen ensured that their achievements would be understood as based on merit rather than devalued as affirmative action.

### DETERMINE YOUR TIME HORIZON

What is your time horizon for this initiative? What will success look like, early on and in the long term? Again, take a balcony view. A gender equity initiative calls for examining deeply embedded norms, values, policies, and habits. Most likely, this change will be incremental over a long period of time. Having an image of success helps focus your strategy and design tactics suited to that image. Sticking to only one image of success may cause you to miss new opportunities and resist  midcourse corrections when unanticipated barriers arise.

### PACE THE WORK

When you're trying to lead change, your own passion and commitment – and even some early success – may inspire you to move quickly. But your pace may be more rapid than the CEO or the system as a whole can absorb.

*Orchestrate the conflict.* Organizational change is a step-by-step process. Make an intervention. Watch and see what happens. Then decide whether to take the next step, hold off for awhile, or make a midcourse correction.

### PRACTICE THE ART OF COMPROMISE

Compromise is a powerful intervention and an important skill in leading adaptive change. *Hold steady.* If you truly understand your environment, you can calibrate when to make an agreement that falls short of your highest aspirations. Here are some things to consider when you are deciding whether to accept half a loaf:

Can you distinguish between what is essential to your issue and what is negotiable, so that you can insist on the former and give up a lot on the latter?

Do your negotiating partners need a small win from you so that they can go back to their board or senior management team without feeling humiliated? You might offer something that you previously insisted on and now are willing to forgo. Or it might be something that is extremely important to your negotiating partners but less important to you.

The reverse is also a factor. Will you go back to your constituents and help them understand why this agreement is okay, even though they gave up some of what was important to them?

Does this "half a loaf" present potential for moving the issue forward fast enough and far enough so that you can revisit it – not too far down the road – and push for more? For example, have you changed a procedure in the CEO search process which may open the door to more progress if it's implemented?

Do your negotiating partners understand that you're willing to accept this smaller change for now, but will expect to engage them in another conversation?

**Hannah Rosenthal**, executive director of the Chicago Foundation for Women and former executive director of the Jewish Council for Public Affairs (JCPA):

For being director of anything, it's essential to bring political skills to the job. Skills of organizing, strategic thinking about who you bring to the table, and the art of compromise. I've tried to figure out how to give something to someone when I'm beating them on an issue, so that there's face-saving. These are things you learn by running political campaigns and political organizing. As an advocate, the hardest challenge is recognizing the importance of compromise, without giving in on values. It was essential for the job I held in the Jewish community.

Resistance is inevitable. Be prepared, as it is likely to arise in both direct and indirect forms.

Remember that the objective of the resistance is to thwart the initiative. The methods will vary but will always be aimed at whatever others perceive as your vulnerabilities. It will be designed to undermine your initiative, even if that means undermining you. Resistance will not come in a straightforward fashion because no one wants to go on record as being against gender equity.

In organizational life, personal attacks are almost always about the message and not, as they appear on the surface, about the messenger. No one is attacked when they are delivering a message that everyone likes, or representing a value that is shared by the group. The attack is a way of diverting attention from the message.

Here are some techniques for dealing with resistance:

**Separate role from self.** Separating role from self is essential, although very hard to do. That's why personal attack is such an effective form of resistance. For example, you may be criticized for your personal style – for being "too single-minded" or "too aggressive." The natural reaction is to respond, but that colludes with the attacker – changing the conversation from advancing women professionals to a conversation about you.

*Take the heat.* When someone tells you that you are being too aggressive or pushy, respond pleasantly and then return to your issue. You need to stay focused, and recognize the pushback for what it is, in whatever form it comes. If you understand that the attack is not about you, but about the issue that you carry, you can deal with it as a function of your role.

**Ruth Messinger**, who assumed the CEO post at the American Jewish World Service after a distinguished career in politics, has remarked:

I pick my battles, figuring out how to get people to listen. Very often when the issue is tough, I spend a lot of time thinking, "What's the best way I can move this?" I'm not saying that men don't strategize, but I think women do it from a perspective that recognizes the stereotypes that affect them. I think women should be pushy and assertive. That's what's needed sometimes. But you need to be aware of the stereotypes about you, to figure out how to make your point, to counter the stereotype without denying who you are.

**Pay attention to skeptics and naysayers.** Skeptics frequently reveal clues about underlying concerns and objections that may be held more widely in your agency. The skeptic will identify holes in your argument and strategy without realizing that he or she is helping you. Treat criticism as valuable intelligence and counsel.

Here's an example: A prominent CEO ushered Shifra into his office waving the *New York Times* article, "The Opt-Out Revolution," by Lisa Belkin, about well-educated women leaving high-profile careers in favor of family life. He proudly informed her that this article gave credence to his own reservations about promoting women. This CEO unwittingly provided Shifra with an important heads-up. AWP's report on bias and gender equity was able to reference this article (and others like it) and counter its arguments with new research findings.

*Think politically.* Maintain relationships with the people who seem most opposed to what you're trying to do. Be in regular contact with them, so that you can read these people, sense how threatening your initiative is, and determine where there might be some room to give. We have also found that, if converted, the most outspoken naysayers can become genuine advocates.

**Watch out for work avoidance.** Resistance also will come in oblique and unanticipated ways. Systems have a way of coming up with subtle strategies to preserve the status quo. The system will generate all sorts of work avoidance mechanisms; for example, someone will suggest that the gender initiative be postponed until after the annual campaign.

Be on the watch for indirect resistance, like someone telling you how terrific your idea is, but then doing nothing to support it or not coming to meetings, albeit each time with a seemingly good excuse. These are all *work avoidance mechanisms* that divert attention from your issue without addressing it directly. Here again, stand back from the fray and get on the balcony so that you can see the patterns and name work avoidance mechanisms when they're being used.

After a local gender equity initiative was created, **Joel Fox**, executive vice president, of the Jewish Community Federation of Cleveland, reflected:

There was no [active] resistance, but there was the same concern that there would be about any new initiative – the fear of not being able to provide the internal resources. This is what our community is famous for. We are famous for enthusiastically adopting new ideas and not providing sufficient internal resources.

Several decades ago, Jewish women volunteers in a close-knit community wanted more attention paid to their leadership potential. They were met with indifference from their male counterparts.

"Why should we change the way we operate?" these men said. "Men are our major donors. Giving them leadership positions makes sense."

"Why should you change?" said one woman. "Because men die first."

Widows are no longer the only females wielding philanthropic clout in the Jewish community. Increasingly, women are taking an equal or primary role in determining family spending and philanthropy. Whether as volunteer leaders of mainstream Jewish agencies or as founders of new organizations, Jewish women are starting to use their wealth to fuel change.

For many years, the efforts to support women in the Jewish world were manifested only as a collection of ideas, articles, and conferences, all intended to influence the people in power.

But, in just one decade, such innovative enterprises as Ma'yan, Kolot, the Jewish Women's Archive, Moving Traditions, and Sharsheret, were launched with major support from women philanthropists. Using philanthropy to institutionalize the movement increases the potential to create systemic change. AWP encourages women donors to use gender equity as a lens to assess whether a Jewish organization is healthy enough to merit philanthropic support.

If you're a professional, you're more likely to create change if you identify and collaborate with volunteer leaders who can provide start-up funding for your effort. Independent funding will give you more independence and credibility. If you're a donor or volunteer leader, don't shy away from making some of your contributions contingent on your agency's willingness to engage in a conversation about gender.

**Barbara Dobkin** has led the way for Jewish women's philanthropy in her support of groundbreaking initiatives that integrate her feminism and her Judaism, including: Ma'yan: The Jewish Women's Project, the Jewish Orthodox Feminist Alliance, AWP, and the Jewish Women's Archive. Here is an excerpt from "Paean to a Troublemaker: Barbara Dobkin" by Letty Cottin Pogrebin, originally published in *Recollections* (Spring 2005):

I want to consider the projects that might never have come to fruition, the work that might never have been accomplished, the people who would never have been energized, inspired, or supported, had Barbara Dobkin never been born...

Barbara has been called many things – smart, tough, indefatigable, funny, brusque, brave, outspoken, and audacious. She functions not just as a donor but as an activist and advocate. She teaches women about money and power. She believes that charitable giving is an opportunity for change-making, and her philanthropic decisions have literally changed the landscape of feminist philanthropy, and put Jewish feminism on the map in concrete ways... Any person or family seeking cues to enlightened philanthropy need only look to Barbara's giving choices.

It is difficult to quantify the combined constituencies and individual beneficiaries of all her life-enhancing, visionary philanthropy. But it's not hard to see the values and the world view at the root of her giving. I'd wager that no other Jewish woman with Barbara's resources has deployed them more mindfully, effectively, or with a greater consciousness of their impact on the future.

---

**Sally Gottesman**, chair of Moving Traditions, is a committed donor-activist, supporting many organizations working at the intersection of gender and Judaism. Here is an excerpt from her article about Jewish women's philanthropy in *Contact* magazine (Winter 2006):

Two years ago, walking through old Jewish graveyards in Poland and Ukraine, I was struck by the fact that women's tombstones, far more than men's, were illustrated with etchings of giving tzedakah. A feminine hand. A coin. A grush being dropped into a box... Women did not pray regularly in shuls; nor did they learn Torah. Consequently, philanthropy was a woman's principal vehicle for religious expression.

With this legacy, why am I often asked to write about the challenge of getting more women to be philanthropists, in a field that has been dominated by men?

Why? Because women are not the "mega-givers," and the mega-givers or even major givers hold the most power... Because of how wealth is distributed in our country, and because these men are generous and because they do care and they do give, these men have enormous influence.

What is behind this question that people ask? Is it a desire to get women's money to support the community – as is? Is there a belief that if women were major philanthropists, something would be different? If women were present at the table, would the issues differ? Would the criteria for funding be altered?

If the answer is the latter, then the prospect of change might be intimidating, both to those at the table and to those who are not. But they – and by this I mean we – need to internalize the idea that women must be at the mega-donor and major-donor tables if we are to build a stronger Jewish community than we have now.

### VALUE YOUR MISTAKES AND FAILURES

Leading an adaptive change is an experiment. If there were a proven formula for sure-fire success, the work of gender equity would have already been done.

Thinking of your initiative as an experiment is liberating. First, you can try several experiments at the same time, so that later you can decide which initiative to pursue with all your resources and which should be dropped. Second, you will be open to assessing the data and making midcourse corrections to incorporate what you have learned.

Thinking about this work as an experiment enables you to learn from the mistakes, setbacks and even outright failures. As in a research lab, every experiment in advancing women professionals is a learning opportunity and a piece of the puzzle. Mistakes then become part of the process rather than a personal blow to the researchers' egos or self esteem.

## MONITORING AND ACCOUNTABILITY

In the nonprofit sector, performance measurement – on both the individual and organizational level – usually hovers informally on the margins, rather than being integrated as a norm. The Jewish community is no exception. In part, this comes from the Jewish emphasis on "saving the world." As a result, Jews often pay less attention to the internal needs of their own agencies.

Another problem is that people often do not want to monitor *or* be monitored – because then they would have to respond and take action. At AWP and CLA, we, too, wrestle with the ongoing challenge of building accountability measures into our client projects and, frankly, using them within our own organizations as well.

### USE ACCOUNTABILITY AS A STRATEGIC TOOL

Accountability is a critical tool that moves a change initiative from *rhetoric* to *being rooted*. If the organization is making a commitment to women's advancement, it must create quantifiable goals that can be monitored and measured. When diversity and women's leadership are articulated in public pronouncements without tangible metrics, it creates a credibility gap.

The best time to advocate for monitoring and accountability is at the start of your gender equity initiative. This might be as modest as a public report on an annual or semi-annual basis, or a committee that is charged to monitor and report on progress. More powerful would be the inclusion of "women's advancement" as a component of performance measurement for senior and middle managers.

Managers who play a role in the change process need to be held accountable. Just as they are evaluated on fundraising and programmatic goals, performance evaluation should assess how they contribute to advancing women in their own departments.

For example, if the salary of the major gifts director depends only on how much money she raised in the previous year, where is the incentive to promote the women in her division? But if there are rewards (and consequences) linked to professional development and promotion of women, the incentives will shift, as will this Director's awareness that her agency is genuinely committed to women's advancement. In this way, the performance review can send a clear message about how the organization values gender equity.

IN OTHER FIELDS
## Systemic Change in the Corporate World

Deloitte & Touche is a professional services firm with corporate and public sector clients in 140 countries. In 2000, then CEO Douglas McCracken set out to increase the number of women partners and to reduce the turnover of women. McCracken was motivated by the bottom line: Deloitte was spending 150% of annual salary to replace each departing female (or male) associate.

What followed was the Women's Initiative, an extensive diversity training program and an overhaul of the firm's consulting structure. The Women's Initiative turned to division managers to give women the career-building assignments they needed to move up the ladder. McCracken demonstrated his commitment to this initiative by including an assessment of progress in each manager's performance review. Results about women's advancement were circulated throughout the firm, and division managers with lagging progress were guided and monitored by senior executives.

Deloitte & Touche has made steady progress in expanding the number of women partners and decreasing turnover. Deloitte has also appointed its first woman Chairman, Sharon Allen.

"Winning the Talent War for Women: Sometimes It Takes a Revolution," McCracken, *Harvard Business Review*, November 2000.

## ASSESS AND USE YOUR OWN RESOURCES

If you are not in a senior authority role, you are not as well-positioned to hold people accountable. But you can still help the organization stay on track.

You or your allies may be viewed as having informal authority on the gender equity issue. Less formal accountability can be useful. For example, if you control some meeting agendas, add gender equity to the topics being discussed. If you are responsible for writing the newsletter, introducing a speaker or moderating a panel discussion, use these opportunities to acknowledge the initiative, applaud senior management, and celebrate signs of success. In the process, you will be reminding your senior colleagues of their stated commitments.

Encourage your colleagues, women and men, to comment on the initiative whenever they have the chance, thus reinforcing the sense, throughout the agency, that the initiative has broad and deep support.

If you or any of your allies are seen as having informal authority on *other* issues, that is also a resource to be leveraged. People who trust you in other circumstances may become new allies as you keep senior leaders focused on the commitment they have made to gender equity.

## IDENTIFY THE SIGNS OF CHANGE

If an organization wants to hold people accountable for their performance on advancing women, there are ways to create incentives and send a clear message. Ideally, this would include such rewards such as higher salaries and promotions. However, even before new performance review structures or incentives are put in place, you and your colleagues can identify the emerging signs of change (or the absence thereof):

- How often does the CEO or board president mention the gender equity initiative?
- How regularly do managers talk to their staff about women's advancement opportunities?
- How is the organization recognizing progress? Announcements at public events? Articles in the newsletter? A personal letter from the board chair?

## SING THE SONG OF ADVANCING WOMEN, AT EVERY OPPORTUNITY

As the gender equity initiative gets underway, inform your community – Jewish and general nonprofit organizations, women's groups, and the media. Applaud the initiative and the public commitment of your agency's leadership. Making the work public is a critical piece in keeping people accountable.

The good news about broadcasting the song of women's advancement is that you will keep the issue alive in your organization and in your community. The not-so-good news is that you risk marginalizing yourself as a one-note singer. The fear of being pigeonholed often prevents women from speaking up and acting on their own convictions. Yet, without strong and powerful voices advocating for change and celebrating progress, we will not close the leadership gap for women. Minimize the possible consequences by monitoring your own job performance, so that the gender equity initiative is not seen as an all consuming passion that diverts you from your core responsibilities. And, at every available opportunity, enlist others to sing the song so that you are not the lone warbler.

# PART III

# Strategies for Change

To achieve gender equity in your organization, you can choose to take action in one or more of these three areas:

- Expanding opportunities for advancement
- Increasing equality in representation and compensation
- Improving the quality of life and work

For each category, we suggest specific initiatives and how you might get started. These suggestions are intended to stimulate your thinking. Be open and flexible. You might think of other initiatives more suited to your organization. Your assessment of the relative merits of each strategy should take into account how long it will take, how risky it is, and how difficult it may be to achieve. We have found that choosing more than one project is a good idea since it's impossible to predict which change effort will take root or have the most impact.

# EXPANDING OPPORTUNITIES FOR ADVANCEMENT

While this guidebook is focused on systemic change, you'll also find recommendations in this section for expanding your own advancement opportunities. Since your ability to support gender equity depends on where you sit in the organization, it may be that the most productive way to close the gap is to move your own career forward. We believe that helping individual women advance creates a more fertile environment for systemic change and at the same time creates a more robust talent pool. That's why we link the two.

Here are several ways for your organization to create the right conditions for women's advancement:

- Identify and cultivate talent.
- Put leadership succession on the agenda.
- Improve the search process.

**Al Miller**, former CEO of FEGS Health and Human Services System, which employs more than 3,500 staff, makes the business case for gender equity:

Leaders who have a "gender problem" when hiring or promoting talent or who waste, lose, or fail to recognize talent, are fools. Talent should be nurtured, mentored, respected, and promoted, male or female. We do this not only because it is the right thing to do but because it is good business practice.

**Gail Magaliff**, current CEO of FEGS Health and Human Services, concurs:

FEGS has a long history of engaging women in senior executive positions. I am very proud that throughout my tenure, individuals have been hired, evaluated and promoted based on demonstrated skill. Our focus is on developing skilled managers and leaders as we support committed and talented staff professionally and personally.

## Identify and Cultivate Talent

Some professions – athletics, music, and dance – have built-in systems for spotting talent. Young people with potential are identified early and given sequenced opportunities to build their skills and hone their craft. Mentoring, practice and performance are central to the development of these future stars.

In most Jewish communal organizations, talent identification and professional development have not been a priority. In part, this is because we are mission-driven and often put human resource development to the side. Women are affected disproportionately by this lack of attention to professional development, given the presence of other gender-based obstacles.

A healthy organization develops its people. This is not only about sending people to training sessions. Supervision, stretch assignments, mentoring and coaching all contribute to cultivating talent. Assessing each person's potential and customizing pathways to help them reach their career goals is essential.

**IN OTHER FIELDS**

**Working Mother** magazine's annual roster of "The 100 Best Companies for Working Women" celebrates companies (based on annual surveys) that support women's advancement through:

- Career counseling
- Mentoring
- Performance management and evaluation
- Leadership training
- Networking groups
- Annual women's leadership conferences
- Formalized executive succession planning

**MAP THE CURRENT LANDSCAPE**

- How is professional development handled within your organization?
- What is the sequence for acquiring skills and expanding the management portfolio?
- Do opportunities exist for job rotations and crosstraining?
- How are women included in training and leadership development initiatives?
- Is there a mechanism for scouting talent in your organization?
- Are the high-potential people identified and cultivated in a systemic fashion?
- What are the pathways to leadership posts; for example, are there "linchpin" positions that must be mastered? (Sometimes this trajectory is assumed rather than stated explicitly.)
- Does the senior management know who their high-potential people are?

## Identifying and Cultivating Talent

These awards and programs promote both women and men. By supporting and showcasing high-potential professionals, they have all contributed to advancing women in the Jewish community.

---

## Awards

The **Covenant Foundation** has led the way by celebrating the contributions of Jewish educators. Covenant annually awards prizes of $25,000 each to three educators and $5,000 to each educator's home institution.

The **Jewish Funders Network**'s J.J. Greenberg Memorial Award honors foundation professionals, aged forty and under, who demonstrate extraordinary leadership in Jewish philanthropy.

The **Jewish United Fund/Jewish Federation of Metropolitan Chicago** gives the annual Samuel A. Goldsmith Award to talented young Jewish communal professionals.

The **Jewish Communal Service Association** gives awards to outstanding young professionals.

---

## Professional Development

The **St. Louis Federation**'s Professional Excellence Project seeks to increase the talent pool, improve staff retention, and make St. Louis a "magnet" for aspiring Jewish communal professionals. Senior and middle managers attend trainings in recruitment, interviewing, supervision, volunteer-professional partnership, and leadership development. The Project, created by local professionals, also offers informal networking and mentoring programs.

---

## Professional Leadership

The **Wexner Graduate Fellowship Program**, established in 1988, is designed to meet the challenges of professional leadership in the North American Jewish Community.

Wexner Graduate Fellows attend graduate school for careers in Jewish Education, Jewish Communal Leadership, the Rabbinate, the Cantorate and Jewish Studies. As Wexner Fellows, they receive financial support, leadership development, and coaching, while participating in a network of their peers.

## ASK FOR WHAT YOU WANT AND NEED

In a project on volunteer leadership, researchers interviewed women board members nationwide, asking them to identify their obstacles and opportunities and what they wanted to do after completing their current board terms. The women usually responded with some variation of the following: "I wouldn't think to ask for anything. I believe that my talents will be recognized and opportunities will come up."

This stood in stark contrast to what we heard from male CEOs of national organizations about their relationships with male volunteer leaders: "When a man comes on my board, he asks me right away about what I have in mind for his future."

Who do you think will be considered first for top leadership posts?

Encouraging women to ask for what they want brings tangible results. Three of the first female presidents of national Jewish organizations campaigned publicly for their offices.

Women professionals benefit when they state their aspirations clearly and enlist their colleagues and supervisors in helping them meet their goals.

**Barbara Balser**, the first woman to become president of the Anti-Defamation League, has said of her election:

I learned that you can't sit back and wait to be asked. You have to go to the kingmakers and offer yourself. My role as development chair had positioned me as a serious national player. People approached me about becoming the national chair. At first I didn't tell anyone that I had decided to run, so I was stunned when another individual asked me to support him for that same position. I didn't realize that people actually approached others and asked for their support!

I made up my mind to tell everybody that I was running. I called eighty people that I knew on the National Executive Committee. I thought that each call would result in a five-minute conversation about my experiences and strengths. But to my great surprise almost every conversation went on for twenty or thirty minutes, answering questions and sharing my vision for the ADL. I did this from morning to night for two solid weeks, making sure to speak to everyone on the Nominating Committee. While not everyone with whom I spoke supported me, I learned that you have to get out there in a big way and talk to people about what you really want and what your mission is. And you will be surprised. People will support you.

Any systematic initiative to identify and nurture high-potential talent will benefit women even if it is not gender-specific.

For example, UJA-Federation has established the Muehlstein Institute at NYU's Wagner School, for high-potential professionals working in the field for less than ten years. To date, 75% of Muehlstein participants have been women.

UJC's Federation Executive Recruitment & Education Program (FEREP) offers graduate school scholarships at prestigious universities in exchange for a two to three year commitment to the Jewish Federation system. Many recipients of FEREP scholarships are women.

Depending on where you sit, you have different ways to introduce talent cultivation:

- If you're on the *senior management team*, put talent spotting on the agenda of your next meeting. Bring a list of the most talented professionals in your organization and encourage your colleagues to do the same. Think about what opportunities can move their careers along.
- If you're a *middle manager*, open a conversation with your peers about creating a system for talent development. What would it take to enlist senior management? Is there a modest, creative way to get it started?
- If you're a *senior volunteer* or *major contributor*, bring the idea for a talent development program to the agenda of your next meeting with the executive or the board … or even underwrite it yourself.

### IN THE JEWISH COMMUNITY
## Women Volunteer Leaders as Allies

Women volunteer leaders can play an influential role in supporting their professional women colleagues. **Terry Meyerhoff Rubenstein**, former chair of the AWP-UJC Gender Equity Team and executive vice president of the Joseph & Harvey Meyerhoff Family Charitable Funds, started a mentoring circle for women professionals at the Associated, Baltimore's federation. The group has met regularly for dinner and discussions on career pathways, supervision, and worklife balance. Each participant in the group has crafted a career plan and is mentored by a leader in the local nonprofit community. In the group's first year, every participant was promoted at least once.

## CULTIVATE A PROFESSIONAL LEARNING ENVIRONMENT

If you are a supervisor, experiment with multiple techniques for cultivating your high-potential women staff:

- Sit down with your supervisees, one by one, and encourage them to articulate the skills they would like to develop. You may not have the resources for a comprehensive plan, but you can pick one or two areas and help your staff expand their capacity.
- Ask senior managers with whom you have a good relationship to allow these women professionals to shadow them for a few days or more.
- Invite high-potential women to important meetings as observers.
- Look for "stretch" opportunities, such as leading a special project or new committee, or participating in a cross-departmental strategy team.

High-potential women need opportunities to learn and practice new skills as they move up the ladder. Support learning opportunities outside the organization.

Make on-the-job learning part of your organizational culture. Debrief after meetings or presentations. Give your staff frequent and honest feedback.

We know of one female CEO in the nonprofit sector who attributes her success, in part, to a harsh performance evaluation after her first year on the job. Because she had kept her agency afloat during a daunting fiscal crisis, she expected praise from the personnel committee. Instead, the chair demanded that she upgrade her financial fluency. For several years after, this CEO kept an accounting textbook on her night table. Over time, with the support and guidance of her board treasurer, she mastered the finances, balanced the budget, and ultimately made her agency financially sustainable for the first time in decades. "If the chair had not been so critical," she said, "I would never have made the commitment."

## SEEK OPPORTUNITIES FOR SHOWCASING

Everyone in an organization has opportunities to showcase others. Depending on where you sit, you can suggest a colleague as a panelist, facilitator, or moderator. Make showcasing part of the everyday culture. Ask a high-potential woman to facilitate a meeting or present the findings of a task force to senior management. When you take an important visitor on a tour of the agency or local community, ask a talented junior professional to join you.

## MAKE MENTORING THE NORM

Women who are still struggling to advance cite lack of access to mentors as a key barrier. Research by Catalyst shows that women who do break through the glass ceiling credit one or more mentors as critical to their success.

In traditional mentoring, a senior executive guides a younger professional, giving feedback, translating the organization's "secret code," and providing access to influential colleagues and clients. The dialogue and personal feedback of these pairings often leads to long-term relationships.

Mentoring can be formal or informal. In some corporations, high-potential professionals are carefully matched with particular senior executives. Other organizations design networking events for junior staff and managers to form mentoring pairs on their own.

If you aspire to a middle or senior-level position, select a role model – male or female – and ask if he or she would be willing to meet with you on a regular basis. If you are a senior manager or a volunteer leader, take the first step; identify a high-potential woman and offer yourself as a mentor. If you are a chief executive, model this kind of behavior and create the expectation that your colleagues do the same.

Some organizations don't have enough mentors to go around. Also, it may not be realistic for one mentor to meet an individual's multiple career needs. The model now includes group mentoring and peer mentoring.

**Mark Terrill**, CEO of the Associated in Baltimore, describes how his former CEO mentored him early in his career:

"I was not consciously looking for a mentor when I came to the Associated in 1989 as a young assistant campaign director. Aside from my desire to serve the Jewish people, my goals were not fully focused, and my ambitions were not fully formed. Darrell D. Friedman reached out to me. He saw my potential and was determined to nurture, develop, and reveal it to me. Darrell was my role model who taught through example; my instructor, who shared what he knew; my coach, who both criticized and encouraged me; and my trusted friend."

POSTSCRIPT: In interviews with women professionals at the Associated, Mark Terrill is lauded for mentoring staff at every level.

The Learning Partnerships at the **Muehlstein Institute for Jewish Professional Leadership** benefit early-career professionals through a network of developmental relationships. The goal is to help the Muehlstein Fellows:

- Identify mentors who can meet their multiple learning needs;
- Assess and articulate their learning needs and goals;
- Develop relationships with potential learning partners;
- Adapt to the changing nature of developmental relationships over time; and
- Evaluate the impact of these relationships on their individual learning goals.

**IN OTHER FIELDS**

**Ernst & Young's Women's PLAN (Partners Leadership Alliance & Network)** supports potential women partners through mentoring and career development. Each participant, assisted by an executive coach, creates a plan based on a 360-degree feedback instrument. A mentor selected from the executive board then works with her to fulfill that plan. Participants and mentors also form groups to provide ongoing career support and guidance to each other.

The Chicago law firm **Sidley Austin LLP** provides mentoring to every associate, male and female. In addition, **Mentoring Circles**, coordinated by the Women's Committee, allow women attorneys to share experiences across working groups, levels, practice areas, and office locations. Mentoring circles are linked to networking activities, including a Women and Leadership Series, women-only receptions, and maternity networking lunches.

Aspiring professionals can reach out to mentors above and below, inside and outside their organizations, to fulfill different purposes. The benefit of this board of advisors is a mosaic of expertise and perspectives.

If you select mentoring as a gender equity initiative, articulate the links between mentoring and organizational effectiveness:

- Mentoring increases the productivity of new staff members, so they can "get up to speed" more quickly and avoid mistakes that otherwise might damage internal and external relationships.
- Mentoring gives professionals greater insight into organizational culture, and helps them develop new skills and knowledge, while benefiting from constructive feedback.

- Mentoring is an effective tool for recruitment and retention, sending a strong message about the company's commitment to its staff.
- Mentoring taps a wider range of leadership talent and identifies high-potential professionals early in their careers.

Mentoring also contributes to the advancement of women volunteer leaders. We have found that women volunteers who become chairs or presidents of their local agencies – such as JCCs and Federations – often attribute their success to the guidance of their agency CEOs. For CEOs, this investment in volunteer leaders is worthwhile because there is a direct benefit to their agencies. Busy people are unlikely to devote time to mentoring solely out of altruism. The challenge is to stimulate the self-interest of these professional leaders, to support their volunteer counterparts. That same desire needs to be stimulated on the professional front, between senior managers and their junior colleagues.

**IN THE JEWISH COMMUNITY**

**The Cleveland Jewish Community Federation** has created a program, "Advancing Women to Leadership," to ensure a healthy percentage of women on all agency boards. To bolster this effort, a pilot project has been launched to mentor from six to ten women volunteers. The mentoring program includes a specific curriculum, and both men and women have been enlisted as mentors.

**ADD COACHING TO THE MENU**

Coaching has exploded as a profession to meet the need for more complex skills at the helm in the business and nonprofit worlds. There is the recognition that developing *emotional intelligence* – the ability to understand and manage yourself and others – is a distinguishing factor for individuals who advance and perform effectively in leadership roles.

Coaches give feedback, holding up a mirror that makes visible both strengths that can be leveraged and gaps that need to be addressed. Expert executive coaches are fluent in diverse approaches to interpersonal communication, strategy, and change management.

Many Jewish communal CEOs are benefiting from one-on-one coaching relationships. The UJC Mandel Executive Development Program offers its participants access to coaches. Rabbis are also turning to coaches; after the Rabbinical Assembly released its study on the challenges faced by Conservative women rabbis, the New York Jewish Women's Foundation provided funding for a coaching initiative. The positive response from women participants in these programs reinforces our opinion that coaching is a core part of executive development and particularly valuable for women professionals.

While it's unlikely that Jewish organizations can provide coaching to senior women professionals over the long term, the intervention of a coach, even on a time-limited basis, can make the difference at a critical juncture.

### BUILD A WOMEN'S NETWORK

Women's networks, both formal and informal, provide a supportive environment for colleagues to share strategies for achievement and advancement. Networks expand contacts and encourage collaboration among professionals.

You can launch a network in one of several ways. You can convene a task force to advise senior management or Human Resources about issues facing women in the organization. Or you might create a more informal network to host social events or a speaker series. Draw your network from all the Jewish agencies in your city, to consolidate resources for learning and mentoring. You might also consider starting a network that brings Jewish professionals together with colleagues from other fields.

### AMPLIFY WOMEN'S VOICES

Experiment with creative strategies that will highlight women's visibility and strengthen their influence.

---

**IN OTHER FIELDS**

The Association of Women Surgeons supports the professional and personal needs of women surgeons from residency through retirement, through a regional mentor network, networking events at meetings of the American College of Surgeons, listservs, research fellowships, and career development resources.

Jewish Communal Professionals of Chicago (JCPC) was founded to enhance skills and knowledge, networking and collaboration. Its SULAM (Hebrew for "ladder") project brings senior staff and volunteer leaders together to address gender equity issues, developing professional skills for female Jewish communal professionals and exploring new models for achieving work-life balance and shattering the glass ceiling. Their publication, "Good Business: A Best Practices Guide to Retaining and Advancing Women in Jewish Communal Service," is available online at www.advancingwomen.org

## Four Ways to Make Women's Voices Heard

The following scenario from a Jewish organization may sound familiar. Women volunteer leaders were troubled by a frustrating situation. On the one hand, they had increased the number of women holding leadership positions on the board. On the other hand, their ideas and voices were absent from the major discussions and deliberations of their organization. Why hadn't the presence of more women on the board altered their experience at these meetings?

The women realized that to have greater impact, they would need to change their behaviors, individually and collectively. Here are a few ideas that have helped these women, and others, make their voices heard:

### STEP UP TO THE MIKE

These women were loathe to rush up to the microphone at large meetings or be the first to speak in board discussions. By contrast, their male colleagues lost no time in making their opinions known. Each woman vowed to speak publicly at the next opportunity. The first time led to a second time and then a third, and the women made a habit of reminding each other to step up to the mike. Over time the cumulative effect was the inclusion of more women's perspectives in discussions and meetings.

### TIMING IS EVERYTHING

A Jewish female president of a major university was asked about her strategies for navigating an environment dominated by male academics and trustees. She responded, "I am neither pushy nor loud. But my timing is impeccable, and I know just when to speak up and make an idea resonate for a group."

Timing is a critical skill. When someone wants to have an impact in a meeting, she will focus not only on *what* she wants to say, but on *when* to speak. Often an idea needs to circulate several times before it can be absorbed and accepted.

## Four Ways To Make Women's Voices Heard

### GIVE CREDIT WHERE CREDIT IS DUE

Many women feel frustrated when their ideas are credited to others. They may be angry about being ignored but feel awkward about reclaiming the authorship of important ideas and recommendations.

A Jewish foundation executive offers a practical approach for changing this dynamic. "You can't take the credit back for yourself. But you can get the credit for another woman in the room. If Barbara is the originator of an idea, but Jim is getting the credit, Sheila can say, "That's a great idea for launching the campaign. I was impressed when Barbara suggested it originally. I'm glad that Jim reiterated it and I, too, want to express my support for Barbara's terrific concept."

If enough women start responding in this way, the power dynamics of these groups will shift markedly, with a more level playing field created for women's ideas.

### WEIGH IN ON THE ISSUES

Women succeed by exceeding expectations; the accepted wisdom is that women need to be twice as good as their male counterparts to neutralize the negative impact of bias. A single-minded drive to succeed may help women advance in their own organizations, but this narrow focus can also be limiting. To exert greater influence on the communal agenda, women need to use their expertise and status as a public platform, whether they write about Israel on the op-ed page of the *New York Times* or play a major role in AIPAC or the American Jewish World Service. There's a lot to be gained from becoming a Jewish affairs pundit.

Equally important is to circulate a list of other women who are qualified to weigh in on the issues. The next time you hear, "Of course, we'd be happy to have a woman speak, but we don't know any woman who knows about...," fill in the blank.

Excerpted from "Seven Ways to Make Our Voices Heard," Bronznick, *Journey*, Fall 2002

# Leadership Succession

A recent study reported that over the next several years, 40% of nonprofit CEOs plan to leave their positions. This same study noted that, in more than half of these nonprofit organizations, neither board nor senior staff is talking about succession planning. This is also the case within the Jewish community where many of the male senior professionals and lay leaders are nearing retirement age.

Succession planning is mostly a top-down phenomenon. Board members and volunteer leaders play an important role in making succession planning the norm in their agencies. If you're in a position to influence planning at that level, then you can use succession planning as a tool for advancing women.

If your organization has invested even modestly in professional development and career pathways, then common sense suggests that senior executives and lay leaders follow up by asking, "What is to become of these high-potential professionals who we are training and mentoring?" Repairing the leaky pipeline – and reversing the brain drain of women from the field – needs to become a priority. In a healthy organization, succession planning drives leadership development, to ensure a "deep bench" of talent over the long term.

Some Jewish organizations are too small or narrowly focused to accommodate everyone's career trajectory over time. In these situations, CEOs and volunteers might consider a "roots and wings" approach, encouraging their talented professionals to move to other agencies to help them grow in new ways and possibly to

**Iris Feinberg**, former co-chair of the UJC National Young Leadership Cabinet and president of the Trillium Group, a medical claims processing company, observes:

For me, Young Leadership was a formative experience. My generation went through business school, medical school, and law school. We were aware of the struggles of women who came before us, and we knew enough to ask to be fast-tracked to leadership. But times are changing. The women coming up now, in their thirties, may not be patient enough to wait. They see no reason to sit on a national committee with forty men, to debate an issue and get no satisfaction. They're not ingrained in the culture of the organized community, and they may not know the right person to get them over the hump in the middle levels of volunteer leadership. So they're leaving the community or not coming in at all.

This is a real challenge in the volunteer community. We need to customize the leadership experience. If we can create customized pathways for the next generation of lay leadership, we may keep young people in the community.

return; for example, to give professionals in planning departments greater exposure to fundraising and vice versa. The challenge is to embrace a more expansive view of succession planning, looking beyond your own agency to build the entire Jewish communal field. This is also true for building volunteer leaders. The Jewish community needs to think system-wide about the best way to deploy its volunteer talent.

While anyone can advocate for new approaches to succession planning, CEOs and board officers are best situated to drive this change. However, enforcing the changes will be an adaptive challenge for your organization if it's accustomed to less transparent hiring practices. Here are the steps involved:

### INTEGRATE SUCCESSION PLANNING INTO THE ORGANIZATION'S STRATEGY

Senior executives can begin to address the leaky pipeline by standing back and taking a longer view. First, analyze your organization's needs over time – three, five, and eight years forward. Simultaneously, analyze the pool of high-potential talent within your organization. What promotions and job rotations will benefit your agency while addressing the developmental needs of your staff?

### BUILD MANAGERIAL ACCOUNTABILITY INTO SUCCESSION PLANNING

As CEO, integrate succession planning into your evaluation of the senior management team. Hold your vice presidents, departmental heads, and HR personnel accountable for developing their own succession plans and showing how women candidates are integrated into their strategies.

### EMPHASIZE INTERNAL RECRUITMENT

If you're a senior manager or are positioned well within HR, experiment with recruitment procedures that send a message about the internal advancement of women as an organizational priority.

Post every job opening internally, inviting current professionals to apply. Make sure that all internal applicants are interviewed. Departmental managers should be rewarded for encouraging their high-potential women to compete for openings, even if it means losing them from their own departments.

## The CEO Search Process

When asked to consider how gender plays into the executive search process, Jewish organizational leaders often ask, "Shouldn't we just choose the best person for the job?"

We all want to believe that we make leadership choices in the context of a strict meritocracy. However, our Jewish communal habits do tend to mirror the gender-biased tendencies in other professions, as well as our own particular prejudices.

In her book *Why So Slow? The Advancement of Women*, the distinguished psychologist Dr. Virginia Valian synthesized her research about the negative effects of "gender schema" on women's advancement. Valian found that the effect of being viewed through a gender lens is that men accrue advantages: "small but numerous molehills that accumulate over time to produce a mountain of advantage for men."

Research in the fields of medicine, law, and academia all indicate that women have to perform better than men in order to be rated equally by their colleagues. For example, in analysis of peer review scores for medical post-doctoral fellowship applications, researchers found that women applicants had to be 2.5 times more productive on average than men to receive the same competence score (Bickel 2001).

In one research study cited in *Why So Slow*, resumes with excellent and equivalent credentials were sent to chairs of 147 university psychology departments. The chairs offered to hire the candidates. Male resumes were offered mid-level posts as associate professors. The *same* resumes with female names were offered entry-level posts as assistant professors.

Given this reality, we cannot assume that leadership searches in the Jewish community are conducted by meritocratic standards that set aside questions of gender.

The search process is an important venue for creating a more equitable and effective approach to leadership selection in the Jewish community. But many search processes are already compromised because so few women occupy prominent roles. Organizations tend to cling to fixed mental models; even with good intentions, some people will find it hard to imagine women in those senior positions.

In fact, many of the women holding CEO positions in the Jewish community established their professional credentials elsewhere.

If Jewish organizations are determined to recruit from the full range of excellent candidates, they will have to correct for their tendency to overlook women who have spent their careers in the Jewish community.

IN THE JEWISH COMMUNITY

### Outsiders as CEOs: Where Did They Come From?

**Ruth Messinger:** CEO, American Jewish World Service – NYC politics

**Karen Barth:** former head, Council for Initiatives in Jewish Education – McKinsey & Company

**Hannah Rosenthal:** former head, Jewish Council on Public Affairs – Health and Human Services, Clinton Administration

**Morlie Levin:** national executive director, Hadassah – RAND Corporation

**Elise Bernhardt:** executive director, National Foundation for Jewish Culture – The Kitchen (contemporary arts organization)

#### EXAMINE EACH PHASE OF THE CEO SEARCH PROCESS

- How does the search process work inside your organization?
- Who is involved? Lay leaders? Search firms?
- Who writes the job description and qualifications?
- What are the referral sources?
- Who interviews finalists?
- How are the professionals involved in the search process?
- At each stage of the process, what procedures help or hinder the advancement of women?

#### REVISE THE SEARCH CRITERIA

How have the search criteria been developed? More than likely, the desired characteristics and skills mirror the person who now holds the position. If the incumbent has been successful, the search committee will find it hard to imagine the job being done another way or performed by a different kind of person; for example, by a woman.

The United Synagogue of Conservative Judaism asked AWP to conduct a pilot project with the goal of improving the search process.

**Maxine Epstein**, Marin region director of the Jewish Community Federation, has written of her experience in seeking an interview for a federation CEO position:

I stared at the photo of two shoes; one a man's shoe, one a woman's shoe. The headline for the cover story of the Northern California Jewish Bulletin, was "Who Will Fill These Shoes?" The article described how there were no "qualified" Jewish communal professionals to "fill the shoes" of the CEO position of the Jewish Community Federation of San Francisco, the Peninsula, Marin, and Sonoma Counties, a position which had remained vacant for at least a year.

In the article, there were three pictures – the current federation president (a man); the head of the search committee (a man); and the immediate past federation CEO (also a man). Did I mention that all the CEOs for the past hundred years of this federation were men? I would like to add that all three gentlemen are truly gifted and dedicated leaders of our community.

Because I am a leader with vision and integrity, because I believe in challenging the status quo in the pursuit of excellence, and because I believe it is time for more of us in middle management do the same... I decided to be bold and to do the unthinkable...to suggest that the search committee might consider me, local Maxine Epstein, for an executive position in our federation.

Let me borrow a phrase from our great crone foremother Sojourner Truth:

"Hey, Ain't I a Candidate? Ain't I a Jewish Communal Professional with over twenty years experience in the field? Ain't I got two master's degrees, a proven track record of successful fund-raising and community building, and love of Yiddishkeit!?"

Doesn't the Jewish world require and demand a woman's presence sitting around the Jewish communal table, envisioning and developing the shifting paradigms required to meet the challenges that face our Jewish Community in this 21st century.?!

After reading the article "Who Will Fill These Shoes?" I went to my closet and opened a box of very nice blue pumps, recently purchased. Around each shoe, I wrapped a copy of the article, my resume, and my vision for the future of this Bay Area Jewish community. I sent one to the president and one to the head of the search committee.

It has been many months since sending off my shoes and my suggestions for shifting paradigms, consideration of flex time, job sharing, and management restructuring that would allow the best of us to succeed. I can honestly say that this dramatic act of arm-waving and quiet shouting, "Hey, I'm right under your noses, and I represent a lot of others like me" made no difference whatsoever. And I kind of miss my shoes.

AWP designed a training program for USCJ regional directors to help them work more effectively with synagogues that were seeking rabbis. One aspect of the program was incorporating CLA's Adaptive Leadership approach that we present in this guidebook. The regional directors were trained to facilitate conversations with search committees about their criteria for the rabbinic position to help them manage the resistance from the committees about considering a woman rabbi.

### OPEN THE CLUB DOORS

We often hear that the old boys' club holds sway over the search process. What can you do to open the club doors? You can encourage women in your agency to apply and guide them through the process. You can network among colleagues, friends, and family to identify qualified women. You can post the announcement with women's organizations in your community. Anyone – manager, staff, volunteer, or donor – can serve as an unofficial recruiter.

Your search committee also should reach beyond the club to include perspectives from women and men, and from younger as well as senior volunteer leaders. You can also involve people outside the search process – to define the criteria, to recruit, and to nominate.

### INCREASE THE POOL

Research cited in Valian's *Why So Slow?* shows that token candidates are judged more harshly in the search process than when they are part of a larger group in the applicant pool.

In one experiment, a woman's resume was judged negatively when it was in a resume pool of 10% women and 90% men.

The same resume was still judged negatively, but less so, when it

**Ruth Messinger**, president of AJWS, recalls of her hiring, after years of service as Manhattan Borough President:

The job and I fell into each other. The board needed someone who was willing to come into an organization in a mess – which men rarely do. This is one of the ways that women can make progress, when things are at a bad pass. Over the last twenty years, a significant number of women have been elected to Congressional seats that were perceived to belong to the other party. At some point, a woman who has toiled for the party says, "Just let me run." And they say, "We can't find any more men, so we'll let her run." And then she wins. I had that experience. I had a name. And my board was willing to accept all of the negatives that came with my name. They took me because the organization was in a mess and I was willing to come in.

was included in a pool of 25% women and 75% men.

However, when that same resume was included in a group of 37% women and 63% men, it was judged favorably.

By encouraging women to apply for openings, you increase the likelihood that a woman will get the job.

## EDUCATE THE SEARCH COMMITTEE

Start a conversation with the search committee to surface their assumptions about women candidates and to encourage new ways of thinking. There is ample research showing how the gender lens subverts what appears to be a meritocratic search process.

Some corporate leaders have observed that when a woman is considered for a new position, the hiring person or search committee usually makes judgments based on her *past achievements*. By contrast, men are frequently assessed for their *future potential*. Is it any surprise that these assumptions favor men over women in hiring?

We present examples of current research in the accompanying sidebar. Bring this tip sheet to your search committee, distribute it to influential people in your organization, post it on your organization's Web site or include it in its newsletter.

## BROADEN THE INTERVIEW PROCESS

While interviews are important, they are inaccurate instruments, in and of themselves, for predicting future job performance. Moreover, women can be placed at a disadvantage in the traditional interview framework. For example, male recruiters for a prominent financial firm found that fewer qualified women candidates progressed past the initial interview phase – when the interview was structured in the traditional thirty-minute format. The reason was that male candidates were able to bond more quickly with their male counterparts. When the recruiters extended the interviews with women to forty-five minutes, the result was an increase in female hires (Meyerson and Fletcher 2000).

Experiment with different approaches to the interview. Ask for written material and short presentations. By offering candidates more ways to showcase their accomplishments and articulate their vision, you will reduce gender bias *and* ensure that the best candidate is selected.

## The Search Process Through a "Gender Lens"

In one study, men and women applied for an engineering job, a field in which men predominate. Resumes were drafted for men and women with information about educational background and professional experience. The research subjects were instructed to rank the relative importance of *education* or *experience* as criteria for selection.

　　The study showed that when a woman candidate presented more work experience and her male counterpart presented more educational credentials, then the subject ranked *education* as the primary criterion for hiring. If the woman candidate presented better educational credentials, and the male candidate presented better work experience, the subjects ranked *experience* as the primary criterion.

"Casuistry and Social Category Bias," Norton, Vandello, et al.,
*Journal of Personality and Social Psychology*, December 2004.

In a Swedish study of postdoctoral fellows, peer reviewers assigned points to job candidates. Despite the progressive character of Swedish society, researchers found that the peer reviewers gave female applicants lower scores than male applicants with the *same level* of scientific productivity. In fact, only the *most productive* women candidates – women whose accomplishments rated a full one hundred points – were judged equally competent to the least productive group of male candidates, men who achieved a score of only twenty points.

"Nepotism and Sexism in Peer Review, " Wenneras and Wold,
Nature Publishing Group, May 1997.

Over the past thirty years, screens have become commonplace in orchestra auditions. During this period, the number of women in top American orchestras has increased by 25%. A principal musician for the Metropolitan Opera commented, "I've been in auditions without screens, and I assure you that I was prejudiced. I began to listen with my eyes, and there is no way that your eyes don't affect your judgment. The only true way to listen is with your ears and your heart."

"Orchestrating Impartiality: The Impact of 'Blind' Auditions on
Female Musicians," Goldin and Rouse, *American Economic Review*, September 2000.

# Building Gender Equity for Conservative Women Rabbis

Rabbi Elliot Salo Schoenberg, international director of placement and associate executive director of the Rabbinical Assembly:

The Conservative Movement ordained its first woman rabbi more than twenty years ago. Our sense from the field was that women were not getting enough opportunities. The Joint Placement Commission wanted to fully integrate female rabbis into congregation placement. Our strategy was to create a "national conversation" about women and the pulpit rabbinate.

We began with data collection since congregations and lay leadership needed to recognize that there was a problem. The study, conducted by Steven M. Cohen and Judith Schor, compared the career tracks of men and women rabbis ordained since 1985 and documented both a placement gap and compensation gap. Their report, "Gender Variation in the Careers of Conservative Rabbis: A Survey of Rabbis Ordained since 1985," was mentioned frequently and prominently in the press.

The Commission then took three steps to push the "national conversation" along. First, when visiting congregations, we mention the study. Then we ask about the search committee: Are enough women represented? We ask the committee about their plans to engage

a woman rabbi. More importantly, we changed the questions about the decision-making process. We now ask, "Name three reasons the congregation is ready to engage a women rabbi at this time." We ask committees to justify their choices for finalists, to reveal where gender has played an unfair role.

Second, we have taken the conversation to the national level. There are more visits to congregations. Our director does presentations on the placement process at regional and national USCJ conventions. The Commission offers solutions to eliminate or reduce the obstacles that women face.

The third step was to rework the search process literature for our congregations. The new material summarizes the gender study and the career tracks of women rabbis.

We are again collecting data. The Joint Commission is tracking statistics about interviewing, searching for, and hiring female rabbis. We want to document the progress and use the data to determine our next step for the national conversation.

# INCREASING EQUALITY

One of the most powerful ways to advance women is to increase their numbers at decision-making tables and in public venues. Ask yourself and your allies: What policies would give many women – not just a symbolic few – the opportunities to be seen in influential roles?

For example, any group representing the agency to the outside world in formal presentations, panel discussions, and media events should include at least 35% women. This is the tipping point for ensuring that the minority presence and voice will be accepted as equal participants, rather than tokens. Certainly publications and Web sites can be monitored so that women are given fair space and coverage.

The goal is to get more women at the table, at every table in the organization. This goal can be achieved in two ways. First, if there's a category for inclusion – for example, a meeting of Jewish religious leaders – hold your organization accountable for including women rabbis. Second, if the category virtually excludes women – for example, a meeting of large federation CEOs – *expand the category*. What about including women who occupy the number two position or women CEOs of large-intermediate federations?

## By the Numbers

You may encounter resistance about setting numerical goals for women's participation. But in a field where women – aside from clergy – represent 70% of the workforce, it is surely possible to identify enough talented women for any slot. And since the research shows that women are held to higher standards of performance than men – 2.5 times – adding women is likely to improve any group of decision-makers, leaders, and experts.

**Steven M. Cohen**, research professor of Jewish social policy at Hebrew Union College-Jewish Institute of Religion, and **Shaul Kelner**, assistant professor of sociology and Jewish studies at Vanderbilt University wrote an op-ed, "Gender Bias Is a Fact of Communal Life," published in the *Forward* (June 2006). Here is an excerpt:

Over the years, we have conducted eight separate studies, both quantitative and qualitative, of gender equity in the Jewish communal world. Wherever we turn we find the same pattern. Women are underrepresented in the lay and professional top leadership of Jewish communal organizations. As professionals, women receive substantially less compensation than men performing equivalent tasks.

Gender bias — discrimination against women — is systemic and pervasive in Jewish life, as it is in the larger society. It is also sad, wasteful, and offensive, especially to American Jews. Since the emergence of the modern feminist movement in America and the subsequent rise of the Jewish feminist movement, sensitivity to gender issues has become a constituent element in the identity of leading American Jews, both women and men.

Like many problems, gender bias in Jewish life can be rectified, at least in part, by recognizing the problem, resolving to fix it, and remedying the issue. In our own personal and professional lives, we also struggle to remain aware of our own gender biases. When asked to speak on panels, we ask about their gender composition. When arranging conferences, research projects, and other professional activities, we think, we count, we invite.

But the first responsibility is to recognize just how deep is the problem, and how widespread is the failure to comprehend the impact of systematic and ongoing bias.

In a wider world and a Jewish world where gender bias is the order of the day, "men of good conscience" — and especially men — can no longer stand idly by. Rather, for reasons of good principle, good politics, and good performance, we must insist upon abiding by the norm of gender diversity as a pre-condition to our personal participation.

**Keynotelist.org** is an online database designed to bring more women to the forefront of intellectual, political, and cultural life in the Jewish community. This strategic tool, created by AWP with the support of The Charles H. Revson Foundation, offers listings and profile pages of Jewish women experts in many arenas. Keynotelist.org is a rich resource for the staff and volunteers of Jewish organizations who want to identify women speakers for public programs and conferences.

### CREATE A PORTRAIT OF THE CURRENT REALITY

- Number of women on committees and task forces
- Number of women making presentations in the community
- Number of women on the dais at public events
- Number of women featured on the Web site or in the newsletter
- Number of women whose photographs appear on the organization's "wall"
- Number of women involved in important meetings

### PUBLISH WHAT YOU LEARN

Often men in senior authority roles in organizations – and sometimes even women in those roles - do not realize how few women sit at the various tables until the information is made public. As Linda Kaboolian, a colleague of Marty's at Harvard's Kennedy School of Government, has said, "The privilege of being privileged is not having to recognize your privilege." Whenever you can document gender imbalance in your agency, make the results known.

### ADVOCATE FOR CHANGES IN POLICY

In some situations, legislation has been a valuable tool for increasing the representation of women. The White House Project, for example, hosted a groundbreaking conference, "Why Women Matter," that brought together women from France, Norway, India, and South Africa – countries that have used legislation to set numerical targets for women's representation on village councils, party ballots, and parliaments. The result was that the number of women serving in these governments increased dramatically.

Similarly, you might consider changes in your organization's bylaws or personnel policies around women's representation. If the adopted policies are specific enough, you will provide a principled benchmark for assessing performance and follow-through. The point here is that long-term initiatives require sustained attention – and a range of tactics – for keeping people focused on the goals.

Equally important, the political organizing required for legislative change lets you test the waters and see who is willing to put their personal capital behind gender equity. You learn a lot when you ask someone to put his or her name on a letter or make a public statement of support.

**David Ellenson**, president of the Hebrew Union College-Jewish Institute of Religion:

When I assumed my post as president of HUC-JIR in 2001, I knew that the College-Institute was committed to the notion of gender equality in principle. After all, HUC-JIR had ordained the first woman rabbi in 1972, and, by 2000, hundreds of women had been ordained. Moreover, a trend toward appointing women as faculty members had slowly begun in the 1990s. This stood in sharp contrast to my own student years during the 1970s, when no woman served on the faculty.

Yet the Board of Governors – charged with oversight responsibility for the institution – remained overwhelmingly male. Only a handful of the fifty-five governors were women, and the Boards of Overseers on each campus had no women as chairs. The vision of equality that informed our institution had yet to be transformed into reality, and the skills and abilities of the female half of our population were being neglected as we attempted to fulfill our mission of providing religious, educational, communal, and intellectual leaders for the Jewish people and the Reform Movement. Such a situation was simply unacceptable. I felt that this lack of women in the governing councils of HUC-JIR had to be redressed immediately for the good of the institution.

First, I resolved to build upon the positive directions that were already underway at the College-Institute prior to my appointment. The trend toward appointing women scholars was continued. Over the past decade, fourteen of the twenty-four new tenure-track appointments have been women.

Indeed, nearly thirty women are now professors at HUC-JIR. The effervescence they create is incalculable, as both our men and women students look to them – as well as their male teachers – as sources of knowledge and creativity. Moreover, women have begun to occupy significant positions in the administration of the College-Institute.

With the support of our board chair, Burton Lehman and the active guidance of Barbara Friedman, vice chair, we determined to transform the Board of Governors. Over the next five years, more than a dozen women were appointed to the Board of Governors, and they have been among our most generous donors and most creative spirits. At present, more than a third of our fifty-four governors are women. One of them, attorney Robin Harvey, assumed the post of chair of our Cincinnati Board of Overseers in 2003, the first woman to serve in such a position. Even more significantly, Barbara Friedman was elevated unanimously to the position of chair of the Board of Governors in 2007, the first time in the 132-year history of Hebrew Union College-Jewish Institute of Religion that a woman has led our institution in this capacity.

In reporting on these developments, I cite the work of HUC-JIR Professor Rachel Adler, whose book, *Engendering Judaism*, captures why this chapter in the ongoing history of HUC-JIR is so crucial. As Rachel writes, Judaism confronts an "ethical task" as it attempts "to reflect and address the questions, understandings, and obligations of both Jewish women and Jewish men." In allowing for the full participation of women in the life of our academy, the College-Institute has surely been blessed and enriched. In so doing, HUC-JIR has just as surely been involved in a religious task that seeks to fulfill the messianic promise of dignity and inclusion that lies at the heart of Jewish faith for men and women alike.

In 2006, the Jewish People's Policy Planning Institute (JPPPI) scheduled a conference of organizational leaders to consider the future of the Jewish people.

No women were invited.

In response to an e-mail protest campaign, more than one hundred communal leaders, scholars, professionals, and volunteers – women and men – wrote to JPPPI Director General Avinoam Bar-Yosef and Ambassador Dennis Ross (conference chair).

**Deborah Lipstadt**, professor of Holocaust Studies at Emory University, wrote an editorial for the Jewish Telegraphic Agency. Here is an excerpt:

The Institute is four years old and the number of women involved in its activities can be counted on one hand – without using all of the fingers…The organizers are now trying to offer rationalizations as to why this happened. They claim that they only invited CEOs and people with policy-planning experience, hence the imbalance. They also are scrambling to invite some women…

How can those planning for the Jewish future be unaware of Ruth Messinger, CEO of the American Jewish World Service, one of those responsible for bringing 100,000 people to Washington recently to protest genocide in Darfur?

Did they not know of Morlie Levin, national ED of Hadassah, whose organization has 300,000 members? What about Lynn Schusterman, one of our most "out-of-the box" philanthropists; Edith Everett, a famed philanthropist and former CEO of Grunthal & Co.; and Phyllis Cook, executive director of the San Francisco Jewish Endowment Fund?

They did not include Ellen Heller, president of the board of the American Jewish Joint Distribution Committee. They ignored or did not know of Susie Gelman, chairwoman of birthright Israel; Elisa Bildner, former chairwoman of the Jewish Funders Network; and Susie Stern, campaign vice chairwoman for the United Jewish Communities Federation umbrella group and campaign chairwoman for New York-UJA Federation…

If these men did not know about these talented women, then they're so out of touch that their deliberations are useless. If they knew about them but chose not to invite them, their judgment is bankrupt and their deliberations equally so.

In either case, the policies they propose for the future will be – at best – irrelevant.

POSTSCRIPT: As of January 2007, JPPPI has added three women to its Board of Governors.

## TAKE EVERY OPPORTUNITY TO BRING MORE WOMEN TO THE TABLE

Hiring a woman CEO will send enormous ripple effects throughout the organization. But it's also important to speak up for women along the way, by recommending them for task forces, as committee chairs, and as faculty members.

These are also *symbolic actions* that send a message about organizational change. Shift a woman from the moderator role to the keynote speaker at a conference. Appoint a woman as the chair of a committee that has previously been chaired by men. Whenever there is a female "first," make sure that it's acknowledged publicly.

## MONITOR PROGRESS

Keep counting. Acknowledge success. Thank the people who add more women to the table. A women's advocacy group in your agency or in the local community might publicly recognize the senior managers and board members who take steps toward gender equity.

Ma'yan: The Jewish Women's Project has been a pioneer, beginning with an effort to mobilize women volunteers and to help them achieve top board positions at major Jewish organizations. Since then, several national Jewish organizations have elected their first woman President, including AIPAC, ADL, the Jewish Agency for Israel, and the United Synagogue for Conservative Judaism.

## SYMBOLS SPEAK VOLUMES ABOUT VALUES

In every organization, symbols communicate what is valued. We know this intuitively when we choose a synagogue, a school for our children, and even where we work. Everything sends a message, from the furniture in the reception area to the art in the hallways.

Look at your organization through the lens of gender equity. In our research, professional and volunteer women reported that the omnipresent "Wall of Men" – photographs of past CEOs and presidents – explicitly conveyed the message that leaders come in one gender (and typically, in only one generation). Similarly, if your agency letterhead does not include among the fundraising dignitaries the Women's Division Chair, your agency is telling the community that women are, literally, not on the same page.

The AWP-UJC Gender Equity Project set a goal to increase representation by women at the General Assembly, with targets of 35% women for plenaries and 50% women as breakout presenters. Through persistent advocacy and active engagement with the professionals and volunteers involved in GA planning, progress has been made. Here are the results for 2001 to 2006.

| 2006 GA - LOS ANGELES, CALIFORNIA | MALE | FEMALE | TOTAL | % MALE | % FEMALE |
|---|---|---|---|---|---|
| Plenary | 16 | 5 | 21 | 76% | 24% |
| Breakout Sessions | 115 | 76 | 191 | 60% | 40% |

| 2005 GA - TORONTO, ONTARIO | MALE | FEMALE | TOTAL | % MALE | % FEMALE |
|---|---|---|---|---|---|
| Plenary | 14 | 8 | 22 | 64% | 36% |
| Breakout Sessions | 111 | 84 | 195 | 57% | 43% |

| 2004 GA - CLEVELAND, OHIO | MALE | FEMALE | TOTAL | % MALE | % FEMALE |
|---|---|---|---|---|---|
| Plenary | 26 | 11 | 37 | 70% | 30% |
| Breakout Sessions | 108 | 95 | 203 | 53% | 47% |

| 2002 GA - PHILADELPHIA, PENNSYLVANIA | MALE | FEMALE | TOTAL | % MALE | % FEMALE |
|---|---|---|---|---|---|
| Plenary | 15 | 4 | 19 | 79% | 21% |
| Breakout Sessions | 140 | 71 | 211 | 66% | 34% |

| 2001 GA - WASHINGTON, DC | MALE | FEMALE | TOTAL | % MALE | % FEMALE |
|---|---|---|---|---|---|
| Plenary | 14 | 2 | 16 | 88% | 13% |
| Breakout Sessions | 140 | 82 | 222 | 63% | 37% |

As we said earlier in relation to counting, you will need to change the category or entrance requirements. If your corridor, conference room, or letterhead only displays past CEOs and presidents, it's time to expand the definition. Stretch the category to promote more inclusive ideas about leadership. This may seem like window dressing, but as these symbols accumulate over time, a new message will be broadcast – that diversity trumps tradition.

### REVISE THE NARRATIVE (AND CHANGE THE ENDING)

What is the story that your organization tells – about its beginnings, accomplishments, and aspirations for the future? Changing the symbols also means shifting the narrative.

Listen carefully at meetings and public events. Extract the stories and folklore from the organizational history. Are the triumphs and inspirational moments tethered only to male "heroes"? Where have women played important roles? How can you rewrite your organization's narrative to include women's voices and achievements? How can you make sure that this becomes a habit within your organization, from the weekly newsletter to the annual report?

**IN THE JEWISH COMMUNITY**

**The Jewish Women's Archive** is changing the narrative of Jewish history by offering resources on hundreds of women and women's organizations. This repository includes manuscripts, primary source materials, and curricula. JWA documents Jewish women's impact on feminism, on the American Jewish community, and on society. www.jwa.org

## Compensation

The gender gap in salary and compensation has been well documented. White women earn seventy-eight cents for every dollar earned by a man; minority women earn even less.

This is as true in the nonprofit field as for Fortune 500 companies. Guidestar reports that in organizations with budgets between $25 million and $50 million, male CEOs earned 24% more than women in median salary. In charities with budgets over $50 million, male CEOs earned 46% more than their female counterparts.

In the Jewish world, the gender gap in salary has been documented in formal studies of JCCs and the Conservative rabbinate. A recent multi-site salary study of six communities – including federation professionals, clergy, and educators – confirmed the gender salary gap between men and women at the higher levels: "Gender gaps in salary operate to the detriment of women in all job categories except clerical work and 'other' day school educator positions (e.g., librarians, guidance counselors, etc.) These differentials persist even when controlling for age, years in organization, graduate degree, supervisory responsibilities, and membership in the organization's senior leadership team" (Kelner, Rabkin, and Saxe 2005).

For women professionals, equitable pay is the essential next step in advancement. But the *adaptive challenges* will be considerable. Can the Jewish community publicly discuss this uncomfortable subject? Can women work together, alongside male allies, to take on salary inequity as a policy issue?

We recognize that collective organizing around compensation runs counter to our Jewish communal culture. We want to believe in the noble ideal that everyone is working for "the cause," not for themselves. In this environment, it is very difficult to make salaries a litmus test of gender equity.

In the corporate world, litigation, or threats of litigation, has served as a lever for correcting inequitable pay structures. However, given the family culture of our Jewish agencies, there is extreme reluctance to confront compensation directly and collectively.

In the best of all possible worlds, organizational leaders would commission studies to quantify the salary gaps among their own

employees. Sometimes this happens, as our earlier examples from
M.I.T. and the Rabbinical Assembly demonstrate. This is the next
frontier. We hope that by writing about this issue, we'll inspire a few
forward-thinking CEOs and volunteer leaders to set an example by
looking at salary equity inside their own organizations.

Compensation equity helps create the link between gender equity
and organizational effectiveness. Transparent, equitable compensation
policies make public the way that all professionals – women and
men – are evaluated and promoted. Success strategies for salary parity
might then be applied to other resources, such as support staff, project
funding, and professional development.

### CLARIFY THE CURRENT REALITY

- What do you know about salaries in your organization?
  What information is available?
- What is the market value of your job and other professional
  positions in your organization and similar organizations in your
  region?

### START A QUIET CONVERSATION

Talk about salaries with colleagues. Women tend to shy away from real
talk about what they're paid. Break the taboo. Think about these
discussions as a political strategy for moving gender equity forward in
your organization.

### LINK THE SALARY ISSUE TO OTHER ORGANIZATIONAL PRIORITIES

If your organization is talking about improving recruitment and
retention of young professionals, you can add pay equity to
the conversation and even suggest a salary survey of comparable
organizations.

### PRACTICE NEGOTIATION SKILLS

In the book *Women Don't Ask: Negotiation and the Gender Divide*,
(Princeton University Press, 2003), Linda Babcock and Sara Laschever
present a range of research studies that show that women ask for less,
negotiate less frequently, and accept less. From this perspective,
asking for a better package does help close the gender gap.

However, other research shows that women need to negotiate

*differently* than their male counterparts because of the resistance to women's self-promotion (Kolb and Williams 2000).

If you're starting a new job or are about to be promoted, investigate the market value of your position and the salary trends of colleagues in other agencies. Presenting the factual data may help your supervisor justify your compensation to the CEO or board.

When entering negotiations for a promotion, start with a concise but compelling case about how the organization has benefited – and will continue to benefit – from your work. Do not assume that your supervisor recalls all your responsibilities and achievements. Consider documenting your roles and accomplishments as part of the presentation.

Promotions are usually construed in terms of new titles and higher salaries. What is being asked of you? What additional resources will be made available to you? Negotiate for sufficient staff, budget, and time to do your job well.

Negotiation is a process. If the first round doesn't go your way – you can let the meeting end and ask to come back for another conversation. Sometimes people feel hurt when a supervisor appears to undervalue their contribution. You have to separate your role in the negotiation from your personal feelings. Reopen the negotiation when you're ready to be at your best.

### IF YOU'RE IN A SENIOR POSITION, USE YOUR CLOUT

Are you or another senior professional willing to put this issue on the management team agenda? Where might you find sympathetic allies at the highest levels? Is there a volunteer leader who can bring the articles and research about the salary gap to the CEO? Should the HR director be asked to sponsor a workshop on negotiation? Are there senior males in top management or volunteers whose daughters or wives work in professional settings and who therefore might be more inclined to address the pay equity issue?

# IMPROVING THE QUALITY OF
# LIFE AND WORK

The conflict between professional and personal life is featured regularly in the media, reflecting the centrality of this issue in modern society. Working people – single, partnered, of all ages, on every professional rung, and in every sector – are pursuing careers while juggling individual and family responsibilities. For dual-career families, single parent households, and the "sandwich generation" caring for both children and aging parents, these conflicts are intensified. The challenges of navigating work and life stretch across gender; however, women still assume two-thirds of all household and family responsibilities.

Some articles have documented the so-called "opt-out" phenomenon – in which well-educated career women exit lucrative careers to spend more time with their families. These reports have ignited a controversy about whether women do, in fact, aspire to leadership. The facts are both sobering and encouraging: Catalyst research shows that 57% of women in senior management roles *do* aspire to be CEOs. Plenty of women in the corporate pipeline have the ambition to rise to the highest echelons.

Nevertheless, over the extended *lifespan* – and extended *career span* – women may take time off. A study published in the *Harvard Business Review* (Hewlett and Buck Luce 2005) found that many women professionals do take the "off-ramp" for an average of 2.2 years. However, while the "opt-out" articles focus on so-called "individual choices" that cause women to leave high-end jobs, the research shows that institutional conditions far outweigh family considerations. Women consistently point to the glass ceiling and rigid policies around work-life issues as their impetus for exit. When these women are ready to return to work, they are starting their own businesses or choosing companies that offer legitimate career development and flexible approaches to work-life balance.

Flexibility in the corporate arena is emerging as an important tool – for recruitment, and retention, and as a strategy for advancing women. Moreover, there is increasing evidence that younger professionals – both women and men – are entering the workplace with explicit demands for work-life balance.

**Workplace Flexibility Takes Many Forms**

**Flexible work week:** Employees determine what time they will begin their workdays to achieve agreed-upon goals in one week.

**Part-time:** Employees reduce schedule and workload to achieve a shorter week.

**Compressed work week:** Employees work longer on selected days in order to have more days off; for example, working forty hours in four ten-hour days.

**Telecommuting:** Employees work from a location outside of the main office, from home or satellite locations. Telecommuting may also be combined with a flexible or compressed work week.

**Job sharing:** Two employees divide one job into two parts, with each person working about half-time. In some cases, two people share the same responsibilities; in others, each person carries distinct responsibilities.

## Challenges and Values in the Jewish Community

### WORKPLACE FLEXIBILITY IS A SIGNIFICANT CHALLENGE FOR THE JEWISH COMMUNITY

We have seen how work-life issues stir deep conflict in Jewish organizations. Because personal connections are critical to Jewish community building and identity issues, there is the enduring belief that *face-time = organizational excellence.* This equation is embedded in the antiquated notion that the "ideal" worker is always available and never quits. In the 21st century, however, organizations that expect 24/7 or 24/6 availability are less likely to recruit, retain, and advance talent of either gender.

When workplace flexibility is rejected outright or permitted only on an ad hoc, individual basis – women may decide to leave the organization. The cumulative effect of these forced choices is that managers start thinking, "Why should I invest in these young women? Most of them leave or get on the mommy track." This creates a climate in which managers feel justified in overlooking women's potential, starting on the day of hiring.

Regardless of how you approach a flexibility initiative, be prepared for a serious conversation – more likely, several – about how women's advancement is constrained by the expectations of "face-time." Your initiative can strive to change this conversation – from who's *opting out* to how organizations can *opt into* a collaborative effort around navigating professional and personal life.

Your goal will be to keep that conversation focused on alternative approaches to organizational excellence. When women are judged on their performance, results, and potential – not on their capacity to work 24/7 – they will be perceived and promoted as valuable assets for Jewish organizations.

### Opt Out or Pushed Out?
### The Untold Story of Why Women Leave the Workforce

In 2006, the Center for WorkLife Law at the University of California, Hastings College of Law, released a report, "Opt Out or Pushed Out? How the Press Covers Work/Family Conflict – The Untold Story of Why Women Leave the Workforce," that exposed the flaws in how newspapers typically cover the reasons that women leave the workforce.

According to the lead author, Distinguished Professor of Law Joan C. Williams, "Too often, the press sends the message that work/family conflict is about professional women who 'opt out.' Our analysis shows that many women do not 'opt out.' They are pushed out by workplace inflexibility, lack of child care, and job discrimination."

The report reviews 119 news articles and provides more accurate ways of telling the story of women's workforce participation, among them:

- Today's workplaces are designed for the workforce of the 1950's, in which male breadwinners were married to housewives who took care of home and children. Today, 70% of families have all adults in the workforce.
- Inflexible workplaces drive women and men into neo-traditional roles. The result is many fathers working longer hours than they would like and many women working fewer hours than they would like.
- The United States cannot maintain its competitiveness if it continues to pay large sums to educate many women who then find themselves "de-skilled" – driven out of good jobs and into less good jobs by inflexible workplaces.
- Stereotyping and discrimination drive men into breadwinner roles and women out of them. Many women quit because they encounter "maternal wall bias": gender bias triggered by motherhood. Such women are not freely opting out – they are being pushed out by gender discrimination.

**Jonathan Woocher**, chief ideas officer of the Jewish Education Service of North America (JESNA), and former CEO:

There can be the perception that flexibility means lowering standards and expectations. The executive challenge is conveying the message that flexibility is not a substitute for performance. We value flexibility as part of creating an environment of high performance. High performance means that people feel they can give their all and will achieve results.

Flexibility will not work if you need to know what's going on every minute in every corner of your organization. For supervisors and executives, it means giving up the illusion that we can control everything.

It's not about control over the work process. It's about concern for the work product. The only way I can do that is by individualizing the evaluations and goals. We are upgrading our performance review process, on a personalized basis, because we recognize that people are working under different circumstances.

## WORKPLACE FLEXIBILITY CONNECTS TO DEEPLY HELD JEWISH VALUES

Work-life balance is usually understood as family-friendly policies. However, our Jewish values encourage us to live multi-dimensional lives, with time for family, spirituality, education, culture, and community. Therefore, flexible work schedules should encompass many individual needs – whether an employee is married, partnered, or single and whether the time is spent caring for a newborn baby or enrolling in a graduate course, coaching the soccer team or training for the marathon, helping an aged parent or volunteering with seniors.

Flexible work arrangements should not create competition for who is the most deserving, nor should these arrangements shift the burden to another demographic. We have heard concerns about flexible scheduling from younger women in Jewish organizations; in particular, the assumption that women without children should always be willing to cover for their colleagues with family responsibilities. Instead, all staff members should be invited to apply for flexibility privileges on an equal basis. The emphasis should be on how to structure the work effectively and measure performance.

# Institutionalizing Flexible Work Arrangements

### ASSEMBLE THE BUSINESS CASE

Before starting, construct the business case for flexibility within your own organization. For example, research by Catalyst shows that, on the *cost* side, flexibility decreases staff turnover and absenteeism; on the *productivity* side, flexibility motivates staff to review work processes, strengthen teamwork, and introduce cross-training – all of which improves organizational effectiveness.

### MAP OUT THE CURRENT CONDITIONS

- How is work-life balance discussed in your organization?
- What are the current policies and practices?
- What informal arrangements exist, if any, that benefit people on an individual basis?
- Would these arrangements be jeopardized if made public?

### LOOK UNDER THE RADAR

Survey colleagues quietly to find out who has an alternative working arrangement. Have some departments instituted flexible scheduling on an informal basis? Start collecting ideas and results – without identifying individuals, if by doing so, you'd cause these staff members to risk losing their privileges. If you find some creative arrangements, bring these people together for a conversation about what they have learned as staff and managers. This is one way to start building a coalition for an organizational recognition of the need for flexibility, and of the benefits that can flow from these alternative arrangements.

### DRAFT AN AUDIT OF YOUR DEPARTMENT'S ACTIVITIES

Think about how time and work intersect in your department. What are the expectations – both explicit and implicit – that govern the workflow?

- Which tasks and projects are tied to the calendar? Which tasks and projects are continuous? Which are more long-range?

- Are staff members expected to be on call? Are people tethered to cell phones and Blackberries? Why?
- Is the work pattern a constant stream of overlapping meetings? How frequently do people attend meetings just to stay in the loop?
- How is more reflective work – such as writing, planning, and evaluation – scheduled and structured?
- Do staff members get rewarded for overwork and responding to crises, rather than for good planning and efficient use of time?

### FOCUS ON HOW THE WORK WILL BE ACCOMPLISHED

Flexibility is not about saying yes to every request. Flexibility is an option, not a right. Flexibility starts with the expectation that everyone is committed to the mission and to the work that needs to get done.

- How can the workday be stretched or compressed without compromising organizational goals?
- How many meetings are truly needed each week to achieve these goals?
- How many staff members need to be present at each breakfast, luncheon, and dinner event? What might be the benefit of rotating participation at these events and briefing each other afterwards?
- How might working at home improve performance on selected tasks and projects?
- How might alternative arrangements help to retain high-potential women who might otherwise leave the organization?

**Lisa Steinfeld Katz**, CFO of the Jewish Federation of Greater Atlanta:

While much of Atlanta is bogged down in a "boys' club" mentality, the Jewish community has made tremendous inroads for women in leadership. To help us take advantage of the best resources, we maintain a flexible work environment, which is more committed to getting the work done than mandating schedules.

Our flex hours allow staff to pick their start times (within reason and with supervisor approval), and many take advantage of this to drop kids off at school or pick them up. We are also amenable to part-time positions. We recognize that job-sharing, particularly in easily parceled positions, actually adds value. The key is to create work solutions that win for employees and the employer alike.

As you think aloud with your colleagues about these questions, look beneath the superficial aspects of these activities. How can you translate *time commitments* into *task commitments*?

## SEEK A TRIAL PERIOD

It may not be clear at the outset which forms of flex-time are appropriate for your organization. Negotiating with senior management for a series of low-risk flex tests may be easier than going for a big policy change.

For example, if you're a manager, start by reducing the urgency of just-in-time communications. You might float a rule that no one is to be called or e-mailed on Sunday except in a genuine emergency. Try it for a month and see what happens. Set limits on how many meetings can be held in a day, or trim existing meetings to the minimum length. Experiment with establishing quiet times during the day or week when people can focus on their work without interruption.

## PROVIDE OFF-RAMPS AND ON-RAMPS

If you're in a policy-making role, consider how flexibility can be integrated over the longer arc of career development. For women on the *off-ramp*, provide networking opportunities to keep contacts current and skills sharp. Continue to cultivate the talent. Put former staff members on the mailing list and provide Web site access. For women ready for the *on- ramp*, extend invitations to events and alert them to job openings.

**Susan Behrend Jerison**, former member of the Hillel Task Force on Work-Life Balance says:

Hillel hires people who are passionate role models. But we have a culture where we're always trying to do more and reach more people. We have a very hard time defining what's "enough." The work is never done because the work is what centers us. It's at the heart of who we are.

AWP convened a national task force at Hillel, including directors and young professionals – men and women – to see how the organization might support better work-life balance. What emerged was the need to make this issue "discussed and discussable." As a result, workshops have been offered at the annual Staff Training Conference, and the personnel self-assessment tool now includes a section on life-work balance. Exit interviews with staff members also reference the work-life balance issue.

Following board approval, Hillel changed its Personnel Code to read:

Hillel recognizes the importance of balancing professional and personal lives. Staff is encouraged to be responsive to their family, religious, and personal commitments and obligations, while at the same time satisfying the requirements of their jobs. Individual, immediate flexibility needs should be addressed as needed by the employee's supervisor. Hillel encourages the development of policies and practices regarding flexible work arrangements, realizing that campuses have varying needs, which require different practices and policies.

**Rebecca Caspi**, senior vice-president, director-general/operations of United Jewish Communities (UJC) Israel and former executive director of Worldwide Human Resource Development at the American Jewish Joint Distribution Committee (JDC):

JDC is trying to create a safe space where we can struggle to find the right balance between our work and our private lives. Many members of our senior staff do this intuitively and proactively. It's on this foundation that we share successes, discuss disappointments, and experiment with new mechanisms that will provide the JDC team with quality of life and fulfillment at work. Some of these mechanisms include:

1. Stretching the limits of technology: investigating options for distance management and investing in them where and when appropriate.

2. Flex-time and alternate career paths, on a limited and experimental basis.

3. Developing a culture of caring about these issues and the challenges our staff face as 21st-century parents and providers.

Because JDC is a global organization, succeeding in key positions requires a "road warrior" approach. We have to be out in the field frequently to stay current with our programs around the world. This is draining on the individual and a challenge for the families left back home. We are experimenting with short-term residencies; in these cases, the staff brings their families along. Our staff is passionate about JDC and welcomes the opportunity to transmit this to their families in a meaningful way.

Also, younger staff select role models whom they think have cracked the code to successful life/work balance. While that may be how it looks from the outside, often it's not at all how it feels from the inside. To help colleagues develop a more complete picture, we are frank – telling them what has worked for us and what hasn't and most important, encouraging them along the way.

## JCSA Networking Parents

In late 2003, the Jewish Communal Service Association brought together three women who wanted to cultivate their professional lives while taking time off to raise young children. They created a network for discussing career development, advocating for family-friendly policies, broadcasting alternative job opportunities in the Jewish community (e.g., consulting), studying articles and Jewish texts, utilizing their skills for volunteer activities, and, ultimately, re-entering the workplace. JCSA Networking Parents has now grown to more than seventy women and men, aged twenty-five to forty-five years, who are staying connected and increasing their likelihood of returning to Jewish communal work.

## Flex Pilot Project at the Jewish Board of Family and Children's Services (JBFCS)

JBFCS is one of the Jewish community's largest employers. Its 3,200 full- and part-time staff, Jewish and non-Jewish, serves clients throughout the NYC metropolitan area. AWP selected them as a pilot site to experiment with gender equity strategies. JBFCS has a longstanding commitment to professional development and its CEO, Dr. Alan Siskind, was an enthusiastic supporter of the initiative.

Initially, the AWP team put the focus of the work on showcasing high-potential women. However, initial interviews revealed that JBFCS wanted to explore flexible work arrangements to help recruit and retain a high-level, diverse staff.

**First Steps:** AWP and Catalyst partnered to design the project and convened an internal JBFCS Task Force. Our team interviewed forty-five professionals at every level – exploring career paths, opportunities for and obstacles to advancement, and current practices around workplace flexibility.

**Technical and Adaptive Challenges:** From the start, we confronted significant obstacles. First, the project was launched at a time when JBFCS faced government budget cuts; the program had to be cost-neutral. Second, the project timeline coincided with union negotiations. Third, there was widespread concern about whether flexibility would be fairly distributed across programs.

**Building Buy-in:** Educating people along the way was essential to the project. We sent a summary of the interviews to all program directors under a cover memo from the CEO. Our team also prepared and distributed a report about workplace flexibility in hospitals to explain how these arrangements have been managed in a similar setting. Our JBFCS staff partners created buy-in by placing articles about the flexibility initiative in the agency e-newsletter.

**Meeting Resistance:** The interviews surfaced best practices around informal flexibility in varied clinical programs at JBFCS. We expected that these staff members would want to showcase their effective teamwork and innovative scheduling. However, many staff did not want to go public, concerned that these ad hoc privileges would be rescinded if brought to light. In working with these challenges, the CEO's continued commitment to the project made all the difference. Also, collaborating with JBFCS staff at the senior and middle levels helped the project team stay aligned with the agency's internal dynamics.

**Preliminary Roll-out:** In Spring 2004, the initiative was launched with a brochure, *A Guide to Workplace Flexibility at JBFCS*, outlining the flexible work arrangements and how staff might take advantage of these new opportunities. Each department and program was encouraged to adapt the initiative to its own needs.

**Flex Pilot Project**, continued

**Initial Results:** During the first year, AWP checked in periodically with JBFCS to monitor the project. Two departments experimented with flex scheduling and staff rotations. Not surprisingly, most program directors took a more conservative approach, concerned that the new policy would "open the flood gates" and encourage staff to take unfair advantage of the agency. However, several departments granted flexible schedules to meet short-term family or educational purposes.

**Alan Siskind**, CEO:

We are creatures of structure. When you're the head of an organization, you fear that things will get out of control. But change is not only an issue for the leadership. It's also an issue for staff. Having choices creates a certain degree of anxiety. If you don't have choices, you can say, "I don't have choices, so I have to live a certain way." When you have choices, sometimes it takes awhile to appreciate those choices and work through the anxiety of them.

**Susan Wiviott**, associate executive director of planning:

At the request of the staff, the HR department and MIS department allowed all staff to change their schedules during the summer months, with each person taking one day off each week. As a trade-off, HR and MIS opened earlier and remained open later to accommodate employees in the residential programs, which operate twenty-four hours a day. At first, people had trouble keeping track of the schedules. It sounds simple to change everybody's schedules. Actually, it was an incredible amount of work, to think through how all the functions could be covered. To make sure that the departments were covered adequately, people had to be cross-trained. That has had a long-term, positive impact. Although there were some glitches, people want to try again, although with some modifications.

**Meryle Mahrer Kaplan**, vice president of advisory services at Catalyst:

There is a huge payoff in flexibility. What we have seen over and over again is improvement in recruitment, retention, and employee engagement. There is no way to quantify what that means – that sense of values being in sync. People are looking for ethical organizations.

**Robin Bernstein**, CEO and president of the Educational Alliance (EA), one of New York City's first settlement houses and now a dynamic network of community and cultural centers, reflects on her path to the top position:

I began working at the Educational Alliance twenty years ago. I had two children under the age of six. I loved my work, but after a few months, I told my supervisor that I would have to quit. The hours were just too much to manage. My supervisor hired an assistant to help me manage the daily operations.

For the next two and a half years, I worked twenty-five hours a week, with a wonderful assistant. After I became pregnant with my third child, I wanted to be home full-time and quit my job. I was home for six months when my former supervisor called. The woman hired to replace me was struggling; would I consult to the EA for eight hours a week, to supervise my replacement and oversee the program?

My eight consulting hours grew to ten and then twelve hours. My replacement left and I returned to my former job, working part-time. For six years, I combined working twenty-five hours at the EA with twelve hours of private practice. I made more money in my practice than in my job; however, my passion was the EA.

Over the next few years, as my children grew, so did my professional responsibilities and my ambition. When my three children were in school, I was offered a very senior position at the agency. I closed my private practice and returned to the EA full-time.

Five years later I became executive director. During this journey, I was made acting executive director for ten months. At the interview, I was asked how I would manage my children and the agency. My response was, "Did you ask my male predecessor the same question?" The question was dropped. But I was not made executive director at that time. The agency brought in a man while I stayed as chief program officer. He was terminated fifteen months later, and I was appointed executive director the next day.

I have been the head of the Educational Alliance for the past eight years. During this time, I have been keenly aware of how the agency's flexibility enabled me to become the CEO. I use that experience in hiring staff and in shaping our culture. I try very hard to provide others with the experience that enabled me to move from being a union employee making $22,800 in 1987 to the head of this $26 million agency. As a footnote, the Educational Alliance is in better fiscal shape than it has been in recent history.

# CONCLUSION

## Creating and Sustaining Change in the Jewish Community

As you project a timeline for your gender equity initiative, you will come up against a paradox. On the one hand, deep-rooted organizational change takes from seven to ten years. Meanwhile, change is happening all around you. This suggests that you have to take risks and grab opportunities even if you are not completely ready or the climate is not exactly right.

Caught between these two realities – the long-term horizon of sustainable change and the just-in-time character of organizational life – chart a middle path. Plot a course between the ideal and the realistic, between what is desirable and what is achievable. You need to focus your attention, your resolve, your allies, and your resources on making your way toward that goal. You have to do more than seed ideas; you have to proceed with strategies and tactics that will give these ideas traction, now and over the long term.

We have identified ten common principles that underlie successful strategies to advance women in every field:

- Acknowledge the bias.
- Measure current conditions.
- Develop a plan.
- Bring in the CEO as a champion.
- Give everyone a part to play.
- Monitor progress.
- Hold people responsible.
- Learn from the resistance.
- Keep communicating the challenge.
- Celebrate small wins…while keeping your eyes on the prize.

These principles echo what you have been reading throughout this guidebook. Here we want to underscore three in particular:

### MONITOR PROGRESS

Remember, the most thoughtful plan and timeline is just today's best guess. It is not chiseled in stone. Be nimble about shifts in alliances, strategies, tactics, and messages. For example, the coalition that is with you on one gender equity initiative may be different from the one that aligns with you on the next. Use outside advisors to help you think through your ideas along the way, ask the tough questions, and suggest midcourse corrections.

### CELEBRATE SMALL WINS

Everyone wants to know what the "promised land" looks like. You need a hopeful story to nourish you and your allies along the way, to bolster morale and to keep the momentum going. Frame the big vision but celebrate the small wins. What counts as a small win? An article in the local press about your gender equity initiative. A "Wall of Women" in your agency's main corridor. A new policy that includes women's advancement in performance evaluation. These modest successes show others that change is possible.

In the Jewish community, gender equity has been the problem that many people prefer would take care of itself. Gender equity is often removed from the agenda of priorities, under the excuse of external crises or urgent agency business. This tendency, along with the typical zigzag nature of organizational change, may sometimes make you feel that you're moving in reverse. Naming the interim victories will replenish you, your allies, and colleagues, and may even soften the hearts of the skeptics.

We are realistic and optimistic. Our vision is to create new opportunities for women and to change the Jewish world. We believe that this work is deeply embedded in the values of our heritage, and in the best interests of the Jewish community. Stay connected to the meaning and mission of what you're trying to accomplish. We hope this guide helps you engage fully in this meaningful and powerful purpose.

## Afterword

As this book goes to press, we have come to understand even more deeply how the challenges of gender equity are linked to broader issues of diversity in the Jewish community, including those faced by younger people, lesbian, gay, bisexual, and transgender (LBGT) Jews and Jews of color.

In April 2007, all three of us played significant roles at a gathering called "The Conference for Change: Inclusiveness and Leadership in the Jewish Community." This extraordinary event brought together 120 leaders in Jewish communal service, philanthropy, and academia to work on practical solutions to create change in our community. (For personal reflections on the conference, see sidebars by Barbara Dobkin and Marcella Kanfer Rolnick.) This conference reminded us of the excitement that comes from launching a grand enterprise.

**Barbara Dobkin**, philanthropist-activist, wrote about her experience at the Conference for Change:

In April I took part in the Conference for Change in Princeton, New Jersey, twenty-four hours focused on "diversity and inclusiveness in the Jewish community." Three lessons from this historic event stayed with me.

The first lesson is about being authentic. The day before the conference, storms flooded New Jersey, and both highways to the hotel were closed. But that next morning everyone showed up – 120 philanthropists, organizational leaders, advocacy professionals, and volunteer leaders. Why did people show up? Because they had been assured that the Conference for Change would be different from the usual plenaries and testimonial dinners.

The organizers – Advancing Women Professionals and the Jewish Community (AWP) in partnership with the Center for Leadership Initiatives (CLI) – worked with the philanthropic sponsors, Angelica Berrie and Lynn Schusterman, to design an intense, roll-up-your-sleeves experience. We arrived, agendas in hand, and for the next twenty-four hours devoted ourselves to brain-storming strategies that can change the way that women, Jews of color, and LGBT Jews are treated in our community.

I have to admit that I was skeptical about whether we would have enough time or the right context to explore all these issues at the conference, especially given the incredible diversity in the room. As it turned out, people were energized by the multiplicity of backgrounds, generations, and perspectives. Everyone was intensely curious and determined to come up with solutions – to increase visibility and acceptance, to expand influence and impact. The excitement was palpable. This was an authentic Jewish community.

The second lesson is about partnering as equals. Each member of the organizing quartet brought valuable resources to the table – intellectual, financial, and social capital.

I'm sure that working this way has its challenges. Our community is not set up for genuine collaboration among equals. But we know that our traditional hierarchies can often leave people's wisdom and expertise on the sidelines. What I saw at the Conference for Change is that, when you give every stakeholder an equal voice, you begin to create a vibrant Jewish ecosystem. I wish I could convey the thrill of seeing one of our most powerful volunteer leaders engrossed in conversation with an LGBT advocate, giving feedback to one another on their action plans. What made that possible was the equal partnership at the top.

The third lesson is about making real change. How often do we leave conferences inspired by good intentions that evaporate the next morning? By contrast, our goal at the conference was to come up with practical action plans that answered essential questions: What am I prepared to do in the next six months? What actions can I take in my

**Barbara Dobkin**, continued

sphere of influence? What will make a difference?

We brainstormed and traded ideas. We drafted action plans, shared them, then revised; 120 people, 120 ideas. They ranged from small steps to large initiatives, from the mundane to the magnificent. We called them out and by making them public, we made them real. People connected to each other's ideas and saw how they might collaborate and combine resources. This was Jewish life at its best, drawing on our collective values and our collective imagination.

These three lessons – being authentic, partnering as equals, and making real change – go to the heart of what made the Conference for Change an historic occasion.

**Marcella Kanfer Rolnick**, a young entrepreneur, philanthropist, and volunteer leader, wrote of the impact of the Conference for Change:

How refreshing and NECESSARY to have a conference in which the Jewish community takes a good, hard look at itself and talks openly about how we can change what about us is NOT a "light unto the nations."

Since becoming parents, my husband, Josh, and I have found ourselves engaged in an ongoing dialogue about what kind of Jewish experience we wish to create for our family. It's ranged from discussions of G!d to day school education to spirituality and religious practice to our relationship with Israel. Since the Conference for Change, this has become leavened with conversations about diversity, exposure, acceptance, and action. How can we be part of the change we want to be manifest as our boys grow into young men and begin to form opinions about the Jewish people, their people? And it's not just for them that we are more enlightened and mobilized – it's for all Jews to find a welcome, alluring home within their Jewishness, to have elevated expectations of, and experiences within, our community.

# TOOLS & EXERCISES

These gender assessment tools have been adapted from the excellent surveys developed by the Johns Hopkins University Committee on the Status of Women and from the evaluation tool used by *Working Mother* magazine to select their annual "100 Best Companies for Working Mothers."

## YOUR ORGANIZATION: THE GENDER PROFILE

To download these exercises, go to AWP's Web site: www.advancingwomen.org.

### A. Data Collection and Analysis

1. Does your organization have an employee database? If so, what information does it include?

2. Is the composition of the professional staff with respect to women reviewed annually? If so, by whom?

3. Is a salary study with respect to women professionals conducted annually in your organization? If so:
   a. Who conducts this study?

   b. How are results reported?

   c. Is there a process for reviewing inequities and taking appropriate action? If so, what is the process?

4. Is an analysis of appointment, promotion, and salary decisions routinely conducted? If so:
   a. Who conducts this analysis?

   _____

   b. How often?

   _____

   c. How are results reported?

   _____

   d. Is there a process for reviewing inequities and taking appropriate action? If so, what is the process?

   _____

   _____

   _____

5. Are formal exit interviews conducted with departing staff members? If so:
   a. Who conducts the interview?

   _____

   b. Are interviews designed to elicit information as to whether gender-related issues played a role in the departure?

   _____

   c. In what ways have exit data been utilized?

   _____

   _____

   _____

   d. To the extent that these reviews take place, are they reported to the staff as a whole? If yes, how is this done?

   _____

   _____

   _____

# B. Gender Assessment Tool

## STAFF

| PROFESSIONAL STAFF | TOTAL | FEMALE | MALE |
|---|---|---|---|
| ALL PROFESSIONALS | | | |
| HIGH-RANK POSITIONS* | | | |
| SENIOR MANAGEMENT TEAM | | | |
| OTHER PROFESSIONALS | | | |

**\*High-rank positions:** CEO, Executive Vice-President or comparable title; COO, Associate Executive Vice-President, Assistant Executive Vice-President or similar title; Chief Financial Officer; FRD Director, Endowment Director, Campaign Director; Planning Director

NOTE: These classifications are drawn from UJC Position Research Reports by Professor Steven M. Cohen. While these positions pertain to federations, we offer them as a guide for ranking jobs in your organization.

## VOLUNTEERS

| VOLUNTEERS | TOTAL | FEMALE | MALE |
|---|---|---|---|
| BOARD CHAIR | | | |
| BOARD PRESIDENT | | | |
| BOARD OFFICERS | | | |
| BOARD OF DIRECTORS | | | |
| COMMITTEE CHAIRS | | | |
| HIGH-RANK COMMITTEES* | | | |
| OTHER COMMITTEES | | | |

**\*High-rank committees:** Executive Committee, Nominating Committee, Budget/Finance Committee, Strategic Planning Committee

# C. Organizational Structures and Mechanisms

1. Does your organization's senior management address the status of women? If so:
   a. In what ways is this issue placed on the meeting agenda?

   _____

   _____

   _____

   b. How frequently is this issue addressed?

   _____

2. In the last three years, what problems have been identified by senior management, respective to the status of women?

   _____

   _____

   _____

3. Does your organization have explicit policies and procedures for promotions? If so:
   a. Does your organization have a document detailing these procedures?

   _____

   b. Is this document available to staff?

   _____

4. Are special efforts made on the senior level (professional or lay) to ensure that women are recruited/selected for leadership roles? If so:
   a. What forms do these efforts take (e.g., a committee or task force)?

   _____

   b. How active and effective have these efforts been?

   _____

   _____

   _____

5.  Do performance reviews and compensation policies monitor and reward managers who help women advance?

_____

## D. Professional and Career Development

1.  Does your organization currently have initiatives to encourage the advancement of women? If so:
    a.  How is the program tailored to the needs of women in your organization?

    _____

    _____

    _____

    b.  Who is eligible to participate?

    _____

    _____

    _____

    c.  How many women have participated in this program?

    _____

    d.  What outcomes have resulted from this program?

    _____

    _____

    _____

2.  Are annual reviews of each professional conducted within each department? If so:
    a.  What form does this take?

    _____

    _____

    b.  Who conducts them?

    _____

    c. Is there a formal protocol for addressing each professional's career development? If so, does this include discussion of the following:
- Clarity and achievability of career goals
- Mentoring
- Access to training
- Access to job rotation
- Access to external opportunities and resources

3. What, apart from the annual review, is done to develop the career skills of professionals?

_____

_____

_____

4. Does your organization offer formal mentoring programs for women? If so:
    a. How many women participate in the mentoring program?

_____

    b. How are mentoring pairs or mentoring groups structured?

_____

_____

_____

    c. What outcomes have resulted from the mentoring program?

_____

_____

_____

5. Does your organization offer networking support for women? If so:
    a. How many women participate?

_____

    b. How is the group organized (e.g., institutionally or community-wide)?

_____

    c. What programs and services does this network provide?

_____

_____

_____

6. How are gender-related issues and problems addressed and resolved on an individual basis?

_____

_____

_____

## E. Work-Life Policies and Practices

1. What is the organizational policy with respect to parental leave?

_____

_____

2. Does your organization offer flexible work arrangements? If so:
   a. How are these arrangements determined?
      _____ Formal HR policy
      _____ Informal agreements

   b. What is the range of flexible work arrangements?
      _____ Informal, occasional flexibility (by the day)
      _____ Temporary, short-range flexibility
      _____ Compressed work week
      _____ Part-time employment
      _____ Telecommuting
      _____ Job-sharing

3. How many professionals over the last five years have taken advantage of parental leave and/or flexible work arrangements?

   MEN _____ WOMEN _____

4. What is the organizational policy, if any, around career advancement for professionals who take parental leave or take advantage of flexible work arrangements?

_____

_____

5. What is the effect of career advancement for professionals who take parental leave or use flexible work schedules?

_____

_____

# F. Environmental Assessment Worksheet

**CLA THINKING POLITICALLY STAKEHOLDER MAP**

The Adaptive Issue: Flexible Work Schedules

| PERSON/ GROUP | RELATIONSHIP TO ISSUE | PREFERRED OUTCOMES | COMPETING LOYALTIES & VALUES | POTENTIAL LOSSES |
|---|---|---|---|---|
| MALE EXECUTIVE | No personal stake | Stability | His vision and priorities | Controversy |
| SENIOR WOMEN | Some would benefit; some would not benefit | Unclear | Their own career advancement; not being seen as feminist | Relationships w/executive and board |
| MALE HEAD OF HR | Has working spouse and small children | Change of policy | EVP uninterested; other issues rank higher | Upset boss |

©CLA 2005

The Adaptive Issue: _____

| PERSON/ GROUP | RELATIONSHIP TO ISSUE | PREFERRED OUTCOMES | COMPETING LOYALTIES & VALUES | POTENTIAL LOSSES |
|---|---|---|---|---|
|  |  |  |  |  |
|  |  |  |  |  |
|  |  |  |  |  |

©CLA 2005

## G. Sample Strategy and Action Plan for Gender Equity Initiative Worksheet

Strategy:  To increase the number of women who are invited to speak in prominent public forums.

| ACTION STEPS | ANTICIPATED OBSTACLES | RESOURCES NEEDED |
|---|---|---|
| If invited to speak at a conference, I will make sure that women are on the panel with me. Moderators don't count! | People will think twice before asking me to speak. And I am concerned about being perceived as a one-note person. | ▪ My list of great women, which I am happy to share.<br><br>▪ Other people who are willing to do this along with me – so that it becomes a standard operating procedure. |

Adapted from Conference for Change PowerPoint presentation created by Shifra Bronznick and Yonatan Gordis.

## Strategy and Action Plan Worksheet

Strategy: _____

| ACTION STEPS | ANTICIPATED OBSTACLES | RESOURCES NEEDED |
|---|---|---|
|  |  |  |

# H. Sample Exercises for Search Committees

**"REASONS NOT TO ENGAGE A WOMAN LEADER"AND NEW WAYS TO RESPOND**

by **Rabbi Eliot Salo Schoenberg**, international director of placement and associate executive director, Rabbinical Assembly

The Rabbinical Assembly has developed new materials to help search committees discuss their readiness for engaging a woman rabbi. This abridged version of the RA's search committee exercise and sample responses to typical concerns and questions can be adapted for many Jewish communal organizations to open up the conversation about women candidates for leadership positions.

**EXERCISE:**
Divide the selection committee into three groups to discuss:

1.  What does our congregation need to do become ready to engage a woman rabbi?

2.  What will change in our congregation if we engage a woman rabbi?

3.  What doubts, concerns, or issues will be raised that will be obstacles to engaging a woman rabbi?

After discussing in small groups and charting the answers, the larger group can convene again to explore the concerns and issues, some of which may be found among the examples below:

## Sample Concerns and Responses

**1. We are not ready for a woman rabbi.** This is the most common response and often an inaccurate one. Congregants are more open to female clergy than the leadership imagines. Congregants are accustomed to encountering women professionals, whether female doctors, lawyers, corporate leaders, or another profession. Sometimes, congregational leaders say this without really having done their homework. Or they say "not ready" as a way to avoid possible conflict. If the congregational leadership thinks that the congregation is not ready, the leadership needs to ask, "What steps do we need to take to get ready?"

**2. Since Conservative Judaism is not fully egalitarian, we do not have to hire a woman rabbi.** One of the glories of our Conservative Movement is that we are a "big tent" that embraces a range of options. Some of our congregations are more egalitarian, some are less. Our rabbis, female and male, are sensitive to the unique culture of each congregation they serve. The Joint Placement Commission respects a congregation's right not to be egalitarian and its right not to feel comfortable with a female rabbi. On the other hand, more than 90% of the congregations in the Movement consider egalitarianism to be a core value. The JPC does expect these congregations to interview women rabbis in keeping with their egalitarian values.

**3. We need a full-time rabbi committed to our congregation. A woman rabbi may not want full pulpit responsibilities because of family priorities. Or she may leave us to become a stay-at-home mom.** Young rabbis, both male and female, are concerned with issues of balancing the demands of work and family. They can help model, for your congregations' young families, how to set boundaries and find healthy balances between work and family commitments.

If your congregation is questioning the commitment or work ethic of a woman rabbi, rest assured that the time and effort women have put into establishing their careers will not be replaced with domestic issues. In addition, women rabbis are well aware of this prejudicial stereotype and understand that even though women rabbis have been ordained for twenty years in the Conservative Movement, they still have to prove themselves. Our experience is that women who go through the arduous process of training to become Conservative rabbis put 110% of themselves into their work and bring all their heart and talents to their position.

In 2004, the Rabbinical Assembly completed a study of the career trends of women rabbis. This study found that women rabbis who leave the pulpit cite job dissatisfaction and gender bias as their reasons, not family demands. If you welcome your female rabbi with a positive attitude and open hearts she will succeed and be with you for years to come.

**4. Engaging a woman rabbi will be disruptive to the congregation. We already have enough conflict here.** Any new rabbi, female or male, who comes to your congregation, will go through a transition period. This is an unsettling time that cannot be avoided, whatever the gender of your new rabbi. Our experience shows that the conflict and disruption has less to do with gender than with clarifying expectations and becoming familiar with a new leadership style. The RA invites you to create a transition committee to manage this crucial period in the life of your congregation. As you know, congregations cannot avoid conflict, but they can learn to manage them wisely.

**5. Women are too emotional! We can't have that here!** The popular media promotes the image of overemotional women, a stereotype conceived by the Greeks. There is no evidence that this stereotype is based in reality. Furthermore, a rabbi is not just an intellectual who preaches stimulating sermons, but a pastor and counselor who relates to the entire person. The rabbi's task is to model Judaism as an organic whole, a system that encompasses our physical, spiritual, and emotional being. The ideal rabbis are in touch with their own emotional lives and comfortable with the emotional lives of their congregants. Congregations regularly tell us that they are looking for an empathic spiritual leader.  Whether male or female, the best rabbi will be aware of the emotional component of life.

**6. This is a man's world, with a hierarchy and a lot of competition, and women leaders just do not fit in this world.** We live in a society which adores clear winners and losers. In fact, the hottest concept in the business world now is about being nonhierarchical. When hierarchical barriers are removed, there is more interaction which allows for better idea development. The biggest companies are looking for ways to flatten their organizational charts. Our Jewish community and texts have been teaching values of equality for many years, ever since the book of Genesis in which we are told that each one of us is created in the divine image. We have the opportunity to model this profound sense of equality by creating institutions that are open to all and by moving away from hierarchical and exclusionary patterns of leadership.

**7. We do not want a woman rabbi because we are a prestigious congregation, and the leaders in our community will not see her or our congregation as a "winner."** It has now been more than twenty years since women have become Conservative rabbis. If you do not interview women rabbis, you will be missing out on some of the most talented and accomplished rabbis of our Movement. Increasingly, these women rabbis bring resumes deep in expertise, and they bring that wisdom and experience to their new positions. They have developed national reputations through their innovative tefillah, writings, and professional accomplishments. These women rabbis will increase the prestige of any congregation that partners with them.

**8. A woman rabbi may expect us to become a "feminist" congregation. A woman rabbi will take us too far to the "left."** Hiring a female rabbi does not automatically define your congregation as a feminist congregation any more than hiring a male rabbi who has lived in Israel defines you as a Zionist congregation. Both male and female rabbis will be sensitive to the unique culture of your synagogue. It is true that a new rabbi will bring changes. The process of making change is a critical transition issue, and the Joint Placement Commission believes that change should be made in a sensitive and caring way by the new rabbi. The JPC teaches that no changes should be made abruptly or unilaterally. The changes should fit into both the history and the culture of the congregation. In particular, rabbis understand that liturgical changes should be made slowly and carefully, in partnership with the congregants.

**9. We engaged a woman rabbi in the past, and it didn't work out. We don't want to make the same mistake again.** We all accept that there are many different kinds of male rabbis, and that having a bad experience with one male rabbi is not an indictment of all male rabbis. Similarly, each female rabbi is unique and a negative experience with one rabbi should not lead a congregation to give up on all women rabbis.

**10. How will our congregation benefit from engaging a woman rabbi?** A female rabbi signifies that your congregation is cutting-edge and exciting, a great message to send to the younger generations in your community. Symbolically, it may mean the congregation wants to head in a new direction or be more inclusive. The popular literature holds that female leaders tend to be more collaborative and less hierarchical. However, the main benefits of having a woman rabbi will come from her own personal strengths and experience, and the partnership she builds with your congregation.

# Resources

**Advancing Women Professionals
and the Jewish Community**
www.advancingwomen.org

**Cambridge Leadership
Associates**
www.cambridge-leadership.com

**Catalyst**
www.catalystwomen.org

**Center for Gender in Organizations,
Simmons School of Management**
www.simmons.edu/som/cgo

**Center for WorkLife Law**
www.worklifelaw.org

**The Hadassah-Brandeis Institute**
www.brandeis.edu/hirjw

**Jewish Orthodox Feminist
Alliance**
www.jofa.org

**Jewish Women's Archive**
www.jwa.org

**Keynote**
www.keynotelist.org

**Kolot**
www.kolot.org

**Lilith Magazine**
www.lilith.org

**Ma'yan**
www.mayan.org

**Moving Traditions**
www.movingtraditions.org

**Tutorials for Change: Gender
Schemas and Science Careers**
www.hunter.cuny.edu/
gendertutorial

**The White House Project**
www.thewhitehouseproject.org

# Bibliography

Adler, Rachel. *Engendering Judaism: An Inclusive Theology and Ethics*. Jewish Publication Society, 1998.

Babcock, Linda, and Sara Laschever. *Women Don't Ask: Negotiation and the Gender Divide*. Princeton University Press, 2003.

Bailyn, Lotte. *Breaking the Mold: Women, Men, and Time in the New Corporate World*. Free Press, 1993.

Belkin, Lisa. "The Opt-Out Revolution." *New York Times Magazine*, 26 Oct 2003.

Bickel, Janet. "Gender Equity in Undergraduate Medical Education: A Status Report." *Journal of Women's Health & Gender-Based Medicine* 10, Apr 2001.

Bronznick, Shifra. "From the Sticking Point to the Tipping Point." *Journal of Jewish Communal Service Association* 79, Fall 2002.

Bronznick, S. "Seven Ways to Make Our Voices Heard." *Journey*. Ma'yan: The Jewish Women's Project, Fall 2002.

Buchanan, Constance H. *Choosing to Lead: Women and the Crisis of American Values*. Beacon Press, 1997.

Catalyst. *Advancing Women in Business: The Catalyst Guide: Best Practices from the Corporate Leaders*. Jossey-Bass, 1998.

Catalyst. *Cracking the Glass Ceiling: Catalyst's Research on Women in Corporate Management*. Catalyst, 2000.

Catalyst. *Making Change: Building a Flexible Workplace*. Catalyst, 2002.

Catalyst. *Making Work Flexible: Policy to Practice*. Catalyst, 1996.

Chazan, Cindy. "'Women Hold Up Half the Sky': An Old Chinese Proverb." *Sh'ma*, Apr 2002.

Chertok, Fern, Leonard Saxe, et al. "Exploring the Impact of the Wexner Heritage Program on the Development of Leadership Capital in the Jewish Community." Cohen Center for Modern Jewish Studies, Brandeis University, 2005.

Cohen, Steven M., and Judith Schor. "Gender Variation in the Careers of Conservative Rabbis." The Rabbinical Assembly, 2004.

Cohen, S. M., Shifra Bronznick, Didi Goldenhar, Sherry Israel, and Shaul Kelner. "Creating Gender Equity and Organizational Effectiveness in the Jewish Federation System: A Research-and-Action Project." AWP-UJC, 2004.

Collins, Jim. *Good to Great: Why Some Companies Make the Leap ... and Others Don't*. HarperCollins, 2001.

Collins, J. *Good to Great and the Social Sectors: A Monograph to Accompany Good to Great*. HarperCollins, 2005.

Cunningham, Cynthia R., and Shelley S. Murray. "Two Executives, One Career." *Harvard Business Review*, Feb 2005.

Duerst-Lahti, Georgia, and Rita Mae Kelly, eds. *Gender Power, Leadership, and Governance*. University of Michigan Press, 1996.

Eagly, Alice H., and Linda L. Carli. "Women and the Labyrinth of Leadership." *Harvard Business Review*, Sept 2007.

Fels, Anna. *Necessary Dreams: Ambition in Women's Changing Lives*. Pantheon Books, 2004.

Fletcher, Joyce K. *Disappearing Acts: Gender, Power, and Relational Practice at Work*. MIT Press, 1999.

Friedman, Dana E. "Supervisors' Guide to Flexibility." Families and Work Institute.

Friedman, D.E. "Workplace Flexibility: A Guide for Companies." Families and Work Institute.

# Bibliography continued

Friedman, Stewart D., Perry Christensen, and Jessica DeGroot. "Work and Life: The End of the Zero-Sum Game." *Harvard Business Review*, Nov/Dec 1998.

Galinsky, Ellen, James T. Bond, and E. Jeffrey Hill. "A Status Report on Workplace Flexibility: Who Has It? Who Wants It? What Difference Does It Make?" Families and Work Institute and IBM, 2004.

Galinsky, E., Erin Brownfield, Lois Backon, and Dana E. Friedman. "Workplace Flexibility: A Guide For Employees," Families and Work Institute.

Goldin, Claudia, and Rouse, Cecilia. "Orchestrating Impartiality: The Impact of 'Blind' Auditions on Female Musicians." *American Economic Review*, Sept 2000.

Goleman, Daniel, Richard Boyatzis, and Annie McKee. *Primal Leadership: Realizing the Power of Emotional Intelligence*. Harvard Business School Press, 2002.

Heifetz, Ronald A. *Leadership Without Easy Answers*. Belknap Press, 1994.

Hesselbein, Frances. *Hesselbein on Leadership*. Jossey-Bass, 2002.

Hewlett, Sylvia Ann, and Carolyn Buck Luce. "Off-Ramps and On-Ramps: Keeping Talented Women on the Road to Success." *Harvard Business Review*, Mar 2005.

Horowitz, Bethamie, Pearl Beck, and Charles Kadushin. "Power and Parity: The Role of Women and Men on the Boards of Major American Jewish Organizations: A Research Report." Ma'yan: The Jewish Women's Project, Nov 1997.

Kelner, Shaul, Michael Rabkin, Leonard Saxe, and Carl Sheingold. "The Jewish Sector's Workforce: Report of a Six-Community Study." Cohen Center for Modern Jewish Studies and Fisher-Bernstein Institute for Jewish Philanthropy and Leadership, Brandeis University, May 2005.

Kegan, Robert, and Lisa Laskow Lahey. *How the Way We Talk Can Change the Way We Work: Seven Languages for Transformation*. Jossey-Bass, 2002.

Klein, Freada Kapor. *Giving Notice: Why the Best and Brightest Leave the Workplace and How You Can Help Them Stay*. Jossey-Bass, 2007.

Kolb, Deborah, and Judith Williams. *The Shadow Negotiation: How Women Can Master the Hidden Agendas That Determine Bargaining Success*. Simon & Schuster, 2000.

Levey, Lisa D'Annolfo, and Meryle Mahrer Kaplan. "The Importance of Being Flexible." *Executive Update*, Sept 2002.

Linsky, Marty, and Ronald A. Heifetz. *Leadership on the Line: Staying Alive through the Dangers of Leading*. Harvard Business School Press, 2002.

McCracken, Douglas. "Winning the Talent War for Women: Sometimes It Takes a Revolution." *Harvard Business Review*, Nov/Dec 2000.

Meyerson, Debra E., and Joyce K. Fletcher. "A Modest Manifesto for Shattering the Glass Ceiling." *Harvard Business Review*, Jan/Feb 2000.

Meyerson, D. E. *Tempered Radicals: How People Use Difference to Inspire Change at Work*. Harvard Business School Press, 2001.

Munck, Bill. "Changing a Culture of Face Time." *Harvard Business Review*, Nov 2001.

Norton, Michael I., Joseph A. Vandello, and John M. Darley. "Casuistry and Social Category Bias." *Journal of Personality and Social Psychology* 87, Dec 2004.

Orenstein, Peggy. *Flux: Women on Sex, Work, Love, Kids, and Life in a Half-Changed World*. Doubleday, 2000.

Plaskow, Judith. *Standing Again at Sinai: Judaism from a Feminist Perspective*. HarperCollins, 1991.

Prell, Riv-Ellen, ed. *Women Remaking American Judaism*. Wayne State University Press, 2007.

Rapoport, Rhona, Lotte Bailyn, Joyce K. Fletcher, and Bettye H. Pruitt. *Beyond Work-Family Balance: Advancing Gender Equity and Workplace Performance*. Jossey-Bass, 2002.

Rapoport, R., and Lotte Bailyn. "Relinking Life and Work: Toward a Better Future." A report to the Ford Foundation based on a research project in collaboration with Xerox Corporation, Tandem Computers, Inc., and Corning, Inc., Nov 1996.

Rhode, Deborah L., ed. *The Difference "Difference" Makes: Women and Leadership*. Stanford University Press, 2003.

Schor, Judith, and Steven M. Cohen. "Centering on Professionals: The 2001 Study of JCC Personnel in North America." New York: JCC Association/Florence G. Heller Research Center, 2002.

Thom, Mary. *Balancing the Equation: Where Are Women and Girls in Science, Engineering and Technology?* New York: National Council for Research on Women, 2001.

Valian, Virginia. *Why So Slow? The Advancement of Women*. MIT Press, 1999.

Weiner, Audrey. "Women in Jewish Communal Service: A Reflection." *Journal of Jewish Communal Service* 94, Fall/Winter 1999.

Weiner, A., and Daniel Wartenberg. "Women in Jewish Communal Service: Can the Goal of Increasing Women in Leadership Roles Become a Reality?" *Journal of Jewish Communal Service* 74, Winter/Spring 1997/98.

Weiner, A. "Women in Jewish Communal Leadership in the 21st Century." *Journal of Jewish Communal Service* 71, Winter/Spring 1995.

Wenneras, Christine, and Agnes Wold. "Nepotism and Sexism in Peer Review." *Nature* 387, May 1997.

Wheatley, Margaret J. *Finding Our Way: Leadership for an Uncertain Time*. Berrett-Koehler Publishers, 2005.

Williams, Joan. *Unbending Gender: Why Family and Work Conflict and What to Do About It*. Oxford University Press, 2000.

Williams, J. "'Opt Out' or Pushed Out?: How the Press Covers Work/Family Conflict." The Center for WorkLife Law, 2006.

Wilson, Marie C. *Closing the Leadership Gap: Why Women Can and Must Help Run the World*. Viking Penguin, 2004.

# Author Biographies

## SHIFRA BRONZNICK

Shifra Bronznick is the principal of Bronznick & Co., LLC, a consulting firm that specializes in launching new initiatives and helping not-for-profits navigate change. She has consulted to a wide range of organizations, including the American Indian College Fund, the Public Education Network, the Fresh Air Fund, Hebrew Union College-JIR, American Jewish World Service, Medicare Rights Center, the Charles H. Revson Foundation, the Nathan Cummings Foundation, United Jewish Communities, and the White House Project. Shifra designed the WHP National Women's Leadership Summits which convened the most influential women in business, government, the nonprofit sector, and academia. In collaboration with Ma'yan, she organized Impact and Influence, a conference for women volunteer leaders of national Jewish organizations. Shifra is also the founder and president of Advancing Women Professionals and the Jewish Community. Previously, Shifra served as executive vice president of Swig, Weiler & Arnow, one of New York's premier commercial real estate firms.

## DIDI GOLDENHAR

Didi Goldenhar is a senior consultant to Bronznick & Co., LLC and serves as a member of the research team of Advancing Women Professionals and the Jewish Community. She has provided organizational expertise to foundations, corporations, and nonprofit organizations, including the Lila Wallace-Readers Digest Fund, the Nathan Cummings Foundation, the Citicorp Private Bank, Synagogue 2000, United Jewish Communities, the Fresh Air Fund, PEN American Center, the Harlem Educational Activities Fund, and the White House Project. Most recently, she has consulted to the NYC Department of Education's Leadership Academy and to the Green Group, a consortium of thirty national environmental organizations.

## MARTY LINSKY

Marty Linsky is cofounder and principal of Cambridge Leadership Associates, a leadership consulting practice serving public, private, and nonprofit clients in the United States and abroad. Linsky has been a faculty member at Harvard's Kennedy School since 1982, except from 1992 to 1995 when he served as chief secretary to the Massachusetts Governor. A graduate of Williams College and Harvard Law School, Linsky has been a journalist, lawyer, and politician. He was the assistant minority leader of the Massachusetts House of Representatives, a reporter and editorial writer for the *Boston Globe*, and an editor of the *Real Paper*. His most recent book is *Leadership on the Line*, co-authored with Ronald Heifetz.